SOS for
the MOM

A Christian Mom's Guide to Managing Emotions

MIRELLA ACEBO

For more information, email lifecoachingbymirella@yahoo.com.

ISBN: (paperback) 979-8-88759-565-8

ISBN: (ebook) 979-8-88759-566-5

ISBN: (hardcover) 979-8-88759-827-7

FOR MORE INFORMATION
AND ADDITIONAL FREE RESOURCES
FROM THE
LIFE COACH MOM:

www.mirellaacebo.com

DEDICATED TO:

My mom and my mother-in-law, Delia Calderon and Marina Acebo, who loved their children unconditionally, until their last breath.

Table of Contents

Introduction:
Who is the "SOS for the MOM" book for?

This book is for the everyday Christian mom brave enough to admit she sometimes struggles with her many emotions. It's for every mother who sometimes *feels* her way through motherhood. Are you that mom? Are you a chronic worrier? Are you overwhelmed? Impatient? Controlling? Do you often feel like you're failing as a mom?

Motherhood is as much experiential as it is experimental. It gives us so many opportunities to feel unfit and inadequate. But the truth is, we learn as we go – and we grow as we go. Each chapter of this book focuses on a different emotion we feel as moms and offers ways to help manage it. This book is filled with real stories from my own life as well as encouraging lessons from Bible moms who've gone before us.

"SOS for the MOM" started as a spin-off idea in my head when I tried to think of ten things I wish I knew ten years ago while raising young kids. I had read my share of parenting books, but the knowledge I gleaned from them didn't seem to be enough. Sure, they may have helped me navigate the external circumstances, but they didn't capture the real struggle of my mom emotions.

I hope my personal stories encourage you. I hope the stories from ancient-day moms in the Bible strengthen you. Most of all, I hope the God of the universe empowers you to be exactly the mom your kids need.

Chapter 1

SOS for the New MOM -
All Moms

(from Eve to present day)

I never wanted to be a mom, but I became one at the age of 29. This is my story.

It was the end of May 2002, I was 40 weeks pregnant and still, no baby. Hence why I was induced two weeks later, on June 6. I spent the afternoon visiting my mom at her skilled nursing facility, which had become her new "home" when I could no longer care for her and was about to have a baby. It's days like that one where the circle of life is clearly visible: one new life juxtaposed with the end of another.

My mom had Parkinson's disease, which is a progressive movement disorder that affects the nervous system as well as other parts of the body controlled by nerves. I remember seeing the early signs; it started with a slight tremor on her right side, some minor stiffness, and balance problems, but it only got worse from there. Although there's currently no cure for the disease, there are medications that can (and did) help. It was the same with her diabetes, high blood pressure, and the breast cancer that had metastasized into her bones. My mom juggled health issues her whole life, and would go on to live three more years like that before she passed away in 2005. Yes, it was hard to lose my mom at the age of 61 (I was 31), but in some ways, it was a relief too. She had suffered for so long. She was ready to go, and I was ready to let her. Well, sort of.

There I was, a new mom of a nine-month-old and a two-year-old, in need of my own mom. Yet, instead I had become my mom's mom, in a way. I'd become her full-time caregiver, and officially part of the Sandwich Generation – a phrase that describes adults who are "sandwiched" between caring for their older parents and younger children. It was a privilege to love and care for my mom in her sunset years, and I wouldn't change that. But at the same time, it was also hard. Really hard. There's a whole new level of emotions that comes with juggling it all. You experience feelings of overwhelm, isolation, sadness, guilt, and burnout, to name a few.

My mom was an incredible role model for me. Her heart for Jesus is what I remember most about her. She was a strong woman of faith and I got to see her put her faith into action every single day, especially during the long, treacherous years at the very end. The qualities that always stood out to me most were her gentle spirit, her good attitude, the way she remained positive and hopeful, and how she never complained – I mean never. That was remarkable to me. *How does one remain so strong in the face of so much suffering?* I wondered. Is this what faith can do? Wow. That changed me. It was during that time when I chose to focus on God and grow in my own faith, and it's been a true game changer ever since. There are still many times I wish my mom were here to help me and teach me how to be a good mom to my kids, but in many ways, she already did.

By the way, before I continue, let me just say that this chapter is *not* just for the new mom with a newborn. No. This chapter is for *all* moms, regardless of the age or stage your kids are in right now. The truth is, as our kids grow up, we do too. We're always learning to be the kind of mom they need in their current stage of life. For example, if you've never parented a toddler, pre-teen, teenager, or young adult before, and now you are, you're new at it! Yes, you come with some experience, but you're also learning and growing too. Each new developmental stage for our kids is a "new mom" season for us, so let's give ourselves some grace for not being perfect. Geesh. Perfection was never God's standard; it's ours.

If you're a "newer mom" – meaning you're a mom of a child born in the digital age – you've likely searched the internet, scrolled the feeds, and watched your share of mom videos on YouTube or other social media platforms. Well, back in the days before technology was a household thing, we pretty much only had one book. I'll rephrase that. *I* only had one book, and it was the oh-so-coveted *What to Expect When You're Expecting.* I remember feeling so proud of myself for actually reading a book cover to cover... that was, until my pediatrician gave me his single most important piece of advice for new moms: "Use that book as a doorstop." Come again? Yep. Those were his exact words. "Babies don't come with a book or a manual; they come with a mother," he said in a gentle, but firm voice. "Be the best one you can be and that is enough." But how? I had no mom of my own to call and now, no book to consult.

You know who else had no mom to call or book to consult? Eve. Yes Eve, the wife of Adam. Eve was the first woman, the first mom, and, contrary to what many people may think, she actually had lots of kids other than Cain and Abel. She didn't have a role model or a wise matriarch to teach her how to raise them all; she was the first. How did she do it? Was she good at it? Did she experience all the crazy hormones and feelings we do today? Did she worry, yell, cry, or cuss? Did she stress out, freak out, and feel lonely and overwhelmed sometimes? Or... was that just me this morning? If you're a mom in any stage, you know exactly what I'm talking about.

I don't need to tell you that being a mom is hard, and there are many reasons why it is. One of those reasons is due to our changing emotions. Did you notice how your emotions (both positive and negative) suddenly intensified the moment you became a mom? If you've raised a child for more than ten minutes, you know. We feel incredible highs we didn't know were possible (next level love, joy, attachment, devotion, etc.), but we also feel incredible lows we didn't know existed (levels of worry, anxiety, stress, sadness, etc.). Our emotions are really hard to manage sometimes, aren't they? Why is that? And why else is motherhood so *hard?*

Since the Fall – the moment sin entered the world through Adam and Eve, moms have struggled and we will continue to struggle. Every person on the planet will struggle; there's no exception. Even the great heroines and moms of faith in the Bible faced some pretty tough situations as new mothers. I have to believe they too dealt with the same emotions we do: worry, overwhelm, loneliness, mom guilt, impatience, and more. We shouldn't be surprised by the challenges we face as new moms. Hardship and pain is expected, and no one is immune. The good news, though, is that God is with us through it all. He helps us grow in ways we otherwise couldn't, or wouldn't, without those very hardships. It's not our comfort God wants to build in each season of motherhood, it's our character. I'm not particularly a fan of going through hard stuff, but as Christian moms, we need to be reminded the hard stuff has a purpose – and it's *never* in vain. I know from my own experience that sometimes, we think we're the only ones who have it hard. But it's never true. Simply talk to another mom and you'll see. Nothing bonds moms faster than our shared struggles. That's where we always find common ground.

This book is filled with encouraging stories of "new" moms – mainly from the Old Testament – who went through some pretty hard things. Each chapter will take a closer look at one or two of them as we dive into their stories: their circumstances and the emotions I imagine they felt at the time. These moms and wives are great examples to us today because we can see their courage, patience, and perseverance on display all while raising their families.

Take Sarah, for example. She became a new mom at 90 years old! I can't even imagine what that was like for her. Her biological clock had long since stopped ticking, yet there she was with a newborn.. And what about Eve? She was the perfect wife; she had the perfect life living in a perfect world... for a time, anyways. It wasn't until after her sin and the Fall that she became a new mom, raising children in a new, sinful world. And we know what happened next – her children turned on each other, one killed the other. Then, there's Hagar. Hagar was a single mom who was abandoned by Abraham in the wilderness with her teenage son. The Bible describes Hagar as sobbing at one point – talk about heavy emotions. There's also Mrs. Noah (Noah's unnamed wife), who survived living in "quarantine" with her family and a circus of animals aboard an ark for over a year. Her kids were grown when she boarded the ark, but she became a "new" mom nonetheless, simply because she and her family had to start over in a new world after the flood. And then there's Hannah (mother of Samuel) and Jochebed (mother of Moses). One was desperate for a child but struggled with infertility while the other released her three-month-old baby into the river to save his life. All of these "new moms" went through their own specific hardships while raising their children, and though many of our circumstances may not be even remotely similar, the point is, we do too. When a new mother's heart awakens after giving birth, it will forever feel things with greater intensity than before.

Moms, doesn't it feel good to experience those high-energy emotions like love, joy, and happiness when it comes to our kids? It feels good when we snuggle our children and cover them with kisses. Those "positive" emotions are a gift, right? Does that mean that when we feel "negative," low-level emotions (like sadness or worry), it's a *bad* thing? No, it doesn't. We shouldn't fear our feelings; they're great things. I'm glad we feel. Emotions are gifts. They remind us we're human beings, having a human experience as we respond to things or people we care about. And we don't just care a little – we care a lot, and we care often! In each new season of motherhood, we care about the welfare of our children. For many new moms, there's automatic awe, excitement, and delight at the birth of a new baby – or... not. Some of us may feel sad, weepy, and overwhelmed by all the sudden changes: the physical, hormonal, and emotional. We're learning to care for new life. We may feel tired all the time or be cranky and tearful for "no reason." Depending on the person, there could be low or high levels of worry, anxiety, and uncertainty that come along with being a new mother. New moms are often living in a perpetual state of "Am I doing this right?" and "What's going to happen next?" The demands are high, and our emotions are even higher. It's no wonder we lose it sometimes!

So how do we keep our emotions in check so they don't dominate us? How can we remain grounded and in control when it feels like our emotions are out of control? Sometimes we need professional help like a doctor, therapist or medication perhaps. That's great. There's no shame in that. But we also need God to help us. He teaches us how to live a Spirit-led life, rather than an emotions-led life. He shows us there's a better way to respond to people and situations around us. God invites us to yield to His Spirit in everything we say and do, and to practice self-control where it's needed. If we're not intentional about making this a daily practice (to the extent that we can), our emotions can easily control us… and usually, not for the better.

I have the cutest dog named Dixie. She's a blend of terrier and Brussels Griffon. Every day I take her on a solid 30-minute walk around my block. Sometimes she's just so excited and raring to go that she's tugging ahead at the furthest point of the retractable leash. I usually have to stop and think, *Wait a minute, who's walking whom? Is she in charge, or am I?* That's when I remind myself, *I'm the human. I can certainly decide to take control.* This is similar to our emotions: Do they lead us, or do we lead them?

Here's where I want to get practical by sharing with you 12 things I think every new mom should know. These apply to brand-new mommies just as much as seasoned mommies who find themselves in a new stage of parenting. This list is both sensible and spiritual in nature, and in no particular order:

1. We won't know everything there is to know about being a mom, and that's okay. Motherhood is a journey and we learn as we go.

2. Whether your kids are babies or teens, trust your instincts. A mother's intuition is typically spot on. Moms have a sixth sense.

3. Don't be afraid to ignore other people's advice. People will always have an opinion on how you should raise your children. Be gracious, thank them, and move on.

4. Our kids cry hard as babies, and at some point, we will too. We might cry from exhaustion or frustration or something else. That's okay. The release feels good.

5. The days are long, but the years go quickly. Enjoy the season you're in now, because seasons change. Our kids become someone new as they grow and you'll likely always miss the past.

6. Your health is important, too. Take care of yourself. Eat. Shower. Walk. Pray. Make time for peace and quiet, and give yourself permission to do less.

7. Find ways to connect with God first, and *then* with your child – whenever possible, as much as possible.

Keep <u>both</u> connections going. It might get harder as your kids get older, but do it anyway.

8. Your body will always do weird things after a baby – not just post-birth, but forever. Talk to friends who are further along than you are and share your concerns. It'll help you feel more "normal."

9. We'll naturally want to compare our kids to others. We can't do this. No two moms are the same, no two kids are the same. Just stop.

10. Accept the help from those who want the best for you. We all need a support system, or at least a single friend to connect with in whatever stage we're in.

11. Encourage other moms you come across and share your wisdom. We all need each other.

12. Ditch perfection and be kind to yourself like Jesus is kind to you. Forgive yourself quickly like Jesus forgives you. Become more like Jesus in every way.

Some of the fondest memories I have of my daughter from when she was little were the times we spent reading together. I don't just mean books – although we read those too. I had a framed poem on the wall near her changing table. She couldn't even read at the time and yet, she'd take her little pointer finger and pretend to read as she recited the poem out loud. I had read it aloud to her so often that she had committed it to memory. The words, from Forest Witcraft, were simple, yet so poignant. They read,

"One hundred years from now, it will not matter what my bank account was, the sort of house I lived in, or the kind of car I drove, but the world may be different because I was important in the life of a child."

This poem was a beautiful reminder for me to really be present with my daughter and to enjoy each moment, especially the ones that seemed small and mundane. My worth and significance didn't come from providing her with big, material things; rather, it came from me being myself, her mom. It came from how I showed up every day – my tone, my attitude, my words, and my corrections. It also came from the ways I showed love, patience, calmness, compassion, gentleness, and so much more. None of these things are material in nature. On the contrary, they're spiritual, and can be given freely. My role didn't require me to be perfect, it asked that I be present, invested, and committed to raising my daughter the best way I knew how.

Take it from me – the new mom (honestly, all moms) will always be tempted to be hard on themselves. We'll be tempted to feel like failures. There's always a mom who's doing things "better" than we are. I want to encourage you, mom, because this is where we put our faith into action. Stand firm in who you are when you're tempted to feel any way that makes you feel less than. So, who are you? I might not know you personally – your strengths, weaknesses, gifts, and talents – but if you're a Christian mom and you've been "born again," as the Bible puts it, you're a new creation in Christ Jesus. This means you're a daughter of the King. You belong to God, and you will never stop being His daughter. You can't be unborn and you can't be uncreated. You are highly favored and He will empower you through His Spirit to be all He's called you to be. That's His promise to you. You're never alone; you don't do this alone because you'll always be His child.

In what area of your parenting are you being too hard on yourself? Where are you tempted to feel like a failure? What lie might you be believing about yourself?

Eve was tempted to believe a lie in the garden. She gave into the lie, acted on it, and faced devastating consequences (that we continue to face today). You might be tempted to believe a lie too – a lie that says you're not a good mom, that you're failing, messing up, or doing it all wrong. It's tempting to believe all these things when the evidence is right in front of you (the messy house, the dirty dishes, the crying child, etc.). But God doesn't put us in places to fail. He didn't make you a mom just to let you fail. He positions us to overcome whatever we're facing *with His help*.

Every day, we have a new opportunity to be still before the Lord and align our hearts to His. Remember who you are and *whose* you are. In your times of greatest doubt – those times you wonder if you matter – remember God created you for such a time as this, to be the mom to your child. You can always thrive exactly where you are. Continue to seek Him and you will find Him. Maybe you want to take a quiet moment right now with the Lord. Invite Him in. Shut out any distractions and receive what He has for you.

What do you sense Him saying to you right now? He often speaks to us in a gentle whisper; we simply need to slow down long enough to hear what He has to say.

Remember Hopscotch? It was far better than Dodgeball and Tetherball, in my opinion. In those other games, you either risked getting hit by a jelly ball or cutting off the circulation to your fingertips. No thanks... I was more of a Hopscotch girl. I loved that game. I want you to picture the outline on the ground. The three single squares, then the double squares. The single and the double. Then, the final single. Imagine yourself hopping through the course on one foot, occasionally on two. How do you feel when you're on one foot? Probably a little wobbly and unstable. It takes balance and coordination to hop, then stand on one foot. How about when you're on both feet? That's where you likely find relief. Why? The obvious answer is, when both feet are on solid ground, there's stability. There's safety. You're grounded and centered and can stand up straight. You reach a place of rest where you can catch your breath before moving on.

What helps you feel grounded and anchored, mom? Try this quick activity: I want you to stand up straight with your shoulders back and feet shoulder-width apart. Lift your chin and close your eyes. Maybe even take a moment to adjust your proverbial crown. Take three deep, cleansing breaths.

Focus on opening up your lungs and chest. Settle into a comfortable rhythm of breathing, and quiet yourself before the Lord. Stretch and relax any tight muscles in your face, shoulders, and neck. Breathe in and welcome His Spirit. Breathe out and exhale one lie you're believing. Continue doing this. Breathe in slowly, then breathe out. Let God speak to you. Practice paying attention to His presence and voice. He wants to speak to you; He longs to connect with you. He wants to remind you of what's true about yourself.

Mom, you are a new creation made in Christ Jesus for good works. You were created to bear fruit – not just any fruit, but *good* fruit. That good fruit is love, joy, peace, patience, kindness, goodness, faithfulness, gentleness, and self-control. You have the ability to become more of all these things; all of them are who you are. We cannot afford to believe lies about ourselves or dismiss what God says is true about us. When we believe lies, they destroy us. That's what happened to Eve. Either we stand with God and believe His truth, or we fall for the endless lies. Both God and the enemy have a different agenda for our lives. God came to give us life. His truth re-defines us and strengthens our identity. The enemy, on the other hand, comes to steal, kill and destroy us. His lies will always make us feel small and insignificant. Who and what you choose to believe matters. We get to choose. Will you choose to believe who God says you are, or who you (in your mind) say you are? The things God says are true about us are truer than what our feelings say are true about us.

Do you remember the 2004 rom-com, *50 First Dates*? It's a love story about Henry (Adam Sandler), a marine veterinarian, who falls in love with an art teacher named Lucy (Drew Barrymore), a woman who suffers from daily memory loss. When Henry learns Lucy has amnesia (and that she forgets him every single night because she has no continuity in her memory, apart from her daily chores), he vows to win her over again and again, each and every day.

The way Lucy remembers things is by keeping a journal. Each morning, she also listens to a tape Henry made, labeled, "Good Morning, Lucy." These things help remind Lucy of who she is and the truth about her life. Some of us need a similar reminder every day. You are loved, and that's the truth. Remember that.

Moms, we're not on our own to figure out this motherhood thing. No matter what we've done, believed about ourselves, or said to ourselves up until now, we can always return to our Maker and our manual (Scripture) for a fresh perspective.

Practice every day to align your heart and mind with God's heart and mind. Let's be moms who are okay with not being perfect and okay with asking for help. It's okay to not have it all together. God promises to help us in every season and become who we could never become on our own. He knows the future versions of us and knows best how to get us there.

When I think back on those final years of my mom's life, I realize how much I grew as a person and how much better I am for having been there for her. I learned how to take care of someone besides myself, be selfless, sacrifice, show patience and kindness, listen well, and so much more. I see now how all of those qualities were exactly what I needed to bring into motherhood. The beauty is that every time I love and care for my kids today, I know I'm connecting with the heart and love of my own mom. What a privilege.

Chapter 2

SOS *for the* Failing MOM - *Eve*

(Genesis 1-4)

On our drive home from the beach the other day, my 17 year-old son said to me, "I'm not holding this against you, but why didn't you push me harder when I was younger? I wish I was good at piano or violin or basketball. I could've been a prodigy!" To which my 19 year-old daughter added, "Yeah... and why didn't you teach us Spanish?"

During this moment, I'll admit I felt a flash of contempt for my son's first comment, but at the same time, I lamented the others. Why *didn't* we push our kids harder? Why *didn't* we make them stick to one thing longer than they wanted? Why *didn't we* teach them Spanish?! After all, my husband and I both grew up bilingual, quickly becoming the unofficial interpreters for our respective families. Isn't it obvious that speaking a second language is a huge advantage? Isn't it obvious it would have given our kids a leg-up in the world? If you're nodding your head in agreement right now, thanks for the guilt trip! I feel it.

So my kids didn't learn another language, or become sports stars. Neither of them are playing classical music in the symphony. I hadn't necessarily given these things much thought before, but my son's sudden remarks stirred something inside me. Did I *fail* my kids? Could I have done more? Pushed them harder? Could I have put in more effort or done things differently? Maybe yes, maybe no. When reflecting on this, it really depends on which aspect of *raising my kids* I focus on. It's easy to make a case in hindsight for all the things we should've, could've, or would've done differently. If I spend too much time agreeing with all the "should haves" from my past, all the things I "failed" to do at one time or another, then I'll always feel like a failure as a mom. I'll be the first to admit that there was a time when "mom guilt" would easily get to me, but not anymore. Somewhere along the way, as I grew more confident as a parent, I refused to hold onto it. Nowadays, I no longer choose to live in a place of lasting guilt or regret over what I seemingly "failed" to do in the past and can't change.

Mom guilt. I wonder if Eve had it. She was the first woman, wife, and mom recorded in the Bible. We all know her story. In the beginning, there was God. God then created Adam and Eve to live in a perfect garden, enjoying a perfect union and relationship with Him and each other. God told Adam and Eve to enjoy all of creation: the earth and sky, the birds and animals, the beautiful sunrises and sunsets, all the seasons and natural landscapes. All of it – well, I take that back. God asked that neither Adam nor Eve do this one thing: eat from one singular tree. They could have the entire beautiful, perfect world if they just left that one tree alone. For a time, everything was glorious... until it wasn't. Again, we know Eve's story. She was tempted by the talking serpent and ate the forbidden fruit. In an instant, her world falls apart. Why? Because in that moment of decision, when faced with the choice between right and wrong based on God's instructions, Eve exercised her free will and did as she pleased, rather than what pleased God. Well, as we know, that choice came with some heavy-duty consequences. We blame Eve for everything now, don't we? Not just for her epic wrong choice, but for all the subsequent wrong choices of the entire human race from that day forward. Eve introduced sin into the world, and she will forever be linked to the most tragic temptation story of all time (a.k.a., "The Fall").

When I really think about her, there's so much I wonder about Eve. For starters, after leaving the garden, did her choice to eat the fruit haunt her for the rest of her life? Was she full of regret, shame, or guilt for what she'd done? How many times did she replay that moment in her head, wishing she'd made a different choice? Did God forgive her? Did she even ask? Did she forgive herself? And later on in her life, when she became a mom and lost one son to the other (when Cain killed Abel), did Eve blame herself in some way for that, too? Did she wonder how she could have raised two completely different sons — one "good" and the other jealous enough to murder? Was that somehow her fault? Had she *failed* her kids as a mom? Did she suffer from some form of "mom guilt" all the days of her life?

If we can learn anything from Eve, it's that we as humans can very easily be led astray by our own (sometimes selfish) impulses to act in ways we later regret. Eve gave into temptation when she ate the fruit. We give into our own temptation all the time.

Sometimes we yell at our kids, our partners, sometimes we even yell at the dog. We say mean things we can't take back. Maybe we act or react from a place of anger and rage, or out of exhaustion and impatience. Perhaps there's conflict or tension in our family that connects back to us. Or maybe we are feeling angry or sad, wishing we could go back in time and make different choices because maybe then, we wouldn't feel like such failures in our present moment. Do you ever find yourself living in the "should haves" of your past? Truthfully, I think we're all tempted in that way, it's so easy to judge ourselves for what we did *back then* using what we know now. We're all Eve, in a sense. We make choices all the time and have to live with the not-so-good consequences, don't we? And though our actions (or inactions) may not be as critical to the future of humankind as those of Eve's, there's no takesies-backsies or redos for us, either. So what do we do? How do we move forward and overcome feeling like a failure when we "get it wrong" or when we don't teach our kids a second language?

First, here's what I want to share with you moms: what we do afterward, what we do in *response* to our "failures" is what truly determines the trajectory of our lives – not the failures themselves. If you stay parked in your failure for too long, you'll get stuck. That's not helpful. If you're a mom who struggles with constant "mom guilt" and you want to learn how to release it, I'm going to tell you how. It comes by walking yourself through the door of forgiveness. That's it. That's the *secret* to NOT feeling like a failing mom (which isn't really a secret, but it can be hard to do). Instead of looking toward our failures to tell us *who* we are and *how* we should feel, we can instead turn to Jesus to remind us what's really true about ourselves. What He says is infinitely more important and life-giving than anything we can say about our past mistakes. Jesus is all about forgiveness. It's what restores our relationship back to Him and it's what ultimately brings us the peace we crave.

The truth is, we're not going to be perfect moms or get everything right all the time. We may not ever measure up to the standards and expectations of other moms, our families, culture, social media, or even Pinterest, and that's okay! This doesn't mean we are failing. If you begin to fall into the comparison trap or constantly judge and blame yourself for getting it "wrong," remember that in a family and in our lives, perfection isn't the goal. Honestly, it should never be the goal. Rather, in all things, our relationship with God is the goal. Forgiveness, reconciliation, and restoration, those are the goals. We can't experience peace with God or within ourselves until we learn to make peace with our failures. Only God can help us with that, because no matter how many times we fail, He is there to help us. He's always ready to take us by the hand and help us move forward, beyond what we deserve. That's called *grace*. And it requires something of us, too – to focus less on our failures and more on His forgiveness. To keep making the choice of turning to Him so that we can walk in freedom every single day.

I wonder if Eve made that choice. I wonder how her relationship with God changed after being cast out of the garden and becoming painfully self-aware of her actions. Did she seek God more because she needed Him more? Did she seek Him less because sin distorts our need for Him and instead makes us want to run and hide? I can't know for sure what Eve did, but I know what we're to do. We're not to fix our eyes on our failures forever, but rather fix our eyes on a good and loving Father who wants to forgive us after we fail. In short, we're to return to our Maker. That's what He wants. That's *all* He wants. You, Mom. He wants *you*. He longs for a relationship with you each time you fall. He wants your heart and mind and devotion after you fail. He wants your contrite spirit and full attention so He can pour out His love, grace, and mercy on you. He doesn't want you holding onto guilt, shame, regret, or your feelings of failure. If you're a Believer, then you are His daughter and a part of His family. You have a seat at His table and can tell him anything and everything. He loves you. He forgives you. He would do anything for you. He would even die for you... Oh that's right, He already did.

In some ways, I think a little guilt is good. We need it. It can be very effective if when we feel it, we change our behavior for the better. Don't we want an internal alarm to tell us when we're off track? Otherwise, we wouldn't think to stop our wrongs; and eventually, we'd be in a world of hurt. The problem as I see it is sometimes our guilt is misplaced, working overtime, or we carry it far longer than we need to. Some of us are blaming ourselves way too much and all too often. Does this sound like you? Do you blame yourself for every little thing, even when it might actually be outside your control? Maybe you feel like everything you do is wrong, maybe you feel overly responsible for too many things and can't keep up. Maybe someone is manipulating you. Whatever has you feeling like a constant failure, it's high time you find out why.

Let's start with some general questions. What is it that causes you to feel guilt all too often? Only you can answer that question. Is the guilt you're feeling connected to something you did wrong, or connected to something *someone else* says you're doing wrong? One has to do with your personal and moral convictions, the other may have more to do with people-pleasing tendencies. If your guilt falls in the first category and you said or did something that was hurtful and damaging to someone else, your conscience is letting you know. Thanks conscience! But what can be done about it? Once it's in the past, all we can do is own it – own your part, apologize and then forgive yourself. Don't defend, justify, excuse, or rationalize your behavior. It's easy to lie to other people about the circumstances surrounding the event(s) in question, but you can't lie to your inner conscience. It'll eat at your soul. "Okay, I did this. I shouldn't have, and I'm sorry. Please forgive me." The fact that you feel remorse and can acknowledge the grief you've caused another person really is a gift.

Do you make it a habit to tell on yourself and apologize when you know you're in the wrong? It's one of the most important things I've learned to do as a mom, especially with my kids. If I'm out of line, I apologize. Sometimes it's on the spot, sometimes it's days afterward if I still have a nagging feeling that won't go away. Again, thank your conscience for not letting you off the hook. Apologizing to our kids (and spouses) when necessary and as often as necessary is a great way to model how to take responsibility for our actions. It also helps our kids learn how to mend relationships, which is a much-needed skill that goes a long way.

Let's switch gears now. Maybe your "mom guilt" has less to do with failing other people and more to do with not doing enough or being good enough at something specific. I often used to feel guilty that my house was a mess – dishes weren't done, the laundry was stacked up, and frankly, I had no desire to lift a finger to make anything better. Oh, and don't get me started about the inside of my car. "How come other moms have it all together and I don't?" They don't. "How come other moms' kids are so well behaved and mine aren't?" They're not. "How come she looks so good and I look like I just walked out of a dumpster?" Because maybe you did.

Boy, is it easy for "mom guilt" to creep in when we compare ourselves to others who are seemingly doing everything right! We can be so hard on ourselves, can't we? Maybe you don't feel thin enough, pretty enough, smart enough. Maybe you're the working mom, the stay-at-home mom, the introvert mom, the I-don't-bake-cupcakes-from-scratch-mom and you feel guilty about it. Maybe you're the "mean mom" because you tell your kids "no." Maybe you can't cook or do crafts, and you're always late to practice or a game. Maybe you hate to volunteer at school and you're the last one to ever sign up to host a classroom party. Do you fit into any of these categories? Are any of these where your guilt comes from?

We need to stop giving in to feeling guilty over the things we're not, and lean into our own individuality and strengths. So you're not good at any of the things listed above… What are you good at? What are some of the good things you are, in fact, doing for your kids and family? What's really important to you? What's your life about? Answering these questions can help bring the clarity you need to shake the feelings of guilt. The truth is, there are only so many hours in a day and not everything can be a priority. We must learn to confidently pick and choose what's most important to us, and what aligns with our top priorities. Only <u>you</u> get to decide what's most important for <u>your</u> family. Not everything carries the same weight in your life, and the priorities you have for your family will most definitely be different than those of other moms. Own it!

Something else that might help is to reframe the way you think about things. What if, instead of saying you're failing, you acknowledge you're growing and developing as a mom? What if what you consider "failing" is actually you acknowledging where there's room for improvement? I'm growing. You're growing. I'm changing. You're changing. With each new day and through every season, with the help of God's spirit, we're growing and transforming into the women and moms we're meant to be. That's what Jesus teaches us. With every passing day, He's making us more whole and complete than we were the day before. He's making us new because our new identity is in Christ. In order to fully embrace this new identity, we must learn to let go of our failures and receive the gifts of forgiveness and transformation. We must learn to see our shortcomings for what they are — opportunities to invite God in so He can speak truth and life into the areas we need Him most. Our failures don't have the final say, He does. Let's not stay "stuck in the yuck," but let God take us by the hand and lead us to new life.

So, what are some practical things we CAN STOP DOING to help us move forward?

Let's STOP:

- Beating ourselves up over and over again about past decisions we can't change.
- Calling ourselves nasty names and using derogatory labels.
- Living in a constant state of lament, wishing things were different.
- Looping the same negative narrative in our mind.
- Condemning ourselves based on a momentary event.
- Resigning ourselves to our failures and remaining in guilt.
- Comparing ourselves to other moms who seemingly "have it all together." – They don't.
- Being so hard on ourselves.
- Allowing "mom guilt" to bully us.

Moms, none of these patterns are healthy. They don't help us or serve us in any way. How long are you going to feel bad about that thing you did one, five, ten years ago? How long will you ruminate on the mistakes you made yesterday? Every time we fill our minds with what we could have, should have, would have done differently, we blame ourselves all over again. We can't let our failures be the loudest voices in the room; those voices are expert at keeping us down and guilt ridden. The longer we stay put in shame, the more comfortable and familiar we become in that spot with that reality. However, we are meant to grow. We are designed to grow up spiritually from wherever we are.

So how can we shift from feeling like a "failing mom" to a "confident mom?"

Here's what we CAN do:

- Be mindful of how we talk to ourselves. Parent ourselves with the same love and care as we would our children. How would you talk to your young child?
- Practice catching and releasing our thoughts like we would a ball, similar to how we play catch or how we would release a fish back into the lake. (My husband fishes, so that's a reference which might just be for me.)
- Get out of the "I should have…" funk. It's a trap.
- Speak God's truth over our lives. Who does He say we are?
- Focus on the bigger picture. What's the big story of our lives telling us?
- Take ownership of our lives, today and everyday. Stop doing what we know is wrong and do more of what is right. Start small.
- Be a student of ourselves. What can we learn from our failures, mistakes, and feelings of inadequacy?
- Stand guard at the doors of our hearts and minds. What are we believing about ourselves? What voices are we listening to?

After Eve's original sin, she hid from God. God went looking for her and asked her a simple question, "Where are you?" This is so significant. It's proof that He didn't abandon Eve. He didn't leave her stuck in her fallen state; He sought after her. He does the same with us. He doesn't abandon us when we sin and do wrong, He promises to always walk with us. So I ask you, Mom, "Where are you?" Where are you in your guilt? Where are you in your failures? What do you wish you could've done differently when it comes to raising your children? What might God be teaching you through that area of growth? What change can you make, starting today?

Eve's life was far from easy once she was outside the perfect garden. She went on to have lots of kids, although the Bible only mentions three by name (Cain, Abel, and later, Seth). Cain was jealous of Abel and killed him. Yes, he killed him. I can't even imagine what that was like for Eve. Losing a child is probably one of the worst experiences a mom can go through, but losing one to violence at the hands of another? Eve essentially lost both sons that day.

I can't help but wonder what Eve felt. Did she retrace all the parenting decisions she'd made up until then and wonder where she went wrong? That to me, seems like the natural response from any mom. "Was it me?" "Was it something I did?" "Where did I go wrong?" We too might be feeling guilty about how our kids turned out, who they are, and the choices they're making. Maybe your kids are prodigals; maybe they're making poor choices. Maybe they've walked away from your family's faith and you're disappointed. Maybe you're hurting. Maybe you think you've failed them. If you're plagued with thoughts of "Where did I go wrong?" and "What could I have done differently?" take those thoughts and release them to the Lord. Be open to what He wants to show you.

One of the main lessons that jumps out at me from Scripture concerning our kids and their choices comes from the story of creation itself. After God created Adam and Eve, He gave them autonomy and free will to make their own choices. God never controlled them, even though He knew how things would turn out. He gave them one rule for their protection, and they chose to disobey. The same thing happens with us as parents every day. We raise our kids the best way we know how, giving them rules and boundaries for their own good. Ultimately though, they choose how they will live. That's the point of parenthood; we're not supposed to control our kids. We are simply supposed to love them, guide them, care for them, and train them up in the ways they should go. Then, we release them to their own decisions and yes, consequences. Ouch.

So Mom, what stood out to you from this chapter so far? Have you gotten some clarity on the nature of your "mom guilt?" Whether it's a big sin that's changed the course of your life or the collective guilt of "not measuring up" over time, here's my final encouragement to you: We are more than any given moment. Yes, we'll be tempted to believe our thoughts and hold onto our past (and present) failures. But here's the truth – God knows your past. He knows what you did and all that you will do, and you are not a disappointment to Him. You are not a screw up. You are not a loser. In His eyes, a surrendered and contrite heart who truly seeks Him is not a failure. You are precious in his sight, as the children's Sunday school song goes. He gave us a way to have a relationship with Him. Let's not squander that by focusing on our failures.

And another thing – In those still quiet moments, when you're reminded of your failures, be brave enough to recognize them. Take responsibility for them. There is no need to hide from them. Be honest about what you've done (or not done), because honesty honors God. Honesty honors truth. Then, ask and receive His forgiveness. Forgiveness is the greatest gift of all; asking God for it should be a daily habit. Do you spend more time recalling your failures than asking for forgiveness? If so, what can help change that?

We can't clean ourselves up on our own. We don't have the ability to wipe our souls and consciences clean. If we could've, we would've done it by now. The truth is, Jesus didn't die for us to walk in failure. He died on the cross so we could walk in freedom – freedom from our past (and present) sin, guilt, regret, mistakes, and failures. His cleansing power is available to us every moment of every day through the gift of confession. Confession isn't about condemning ourselves over and over again for what we've done, it's about recognizing when we're off track. It's about, essentially, telling on ourselves, acknowledging we did something that wasn't right and reflecting on how to grow in the future. It's an opportunity to ask for forgiveness and be released from the guilt and shame that weighs us down. Take a moment to confess any failure(s) right now. Do this every day. It's a daily habit we all need, because we all sin daily.

The God who walked with Eve walks with us too. He doesn't run, He doesn't play hide-and-seek. He wants us to seek Him, always. If we're returning to our Maker in all things and giving ourselves back to Him, then we're hardly failing at all. If you *really* want to know if you're failing, here's one final list to ponder. Are you...

Failing to release the things that weigh you down?

Failing to ask for forgiveness on a regular basis?

Failing to embrace God's forgiveness daily and move on?

Failing to forgive yourself?

Failing to trust Him with your sin and shame?

Failing to renew your mind through His word and in prayer?

Failing to accept His mercy and grace?

Failing to love others and love God as He deserves?

Failing to consider His will and way when making choices?

There's so much that makes you, *you*. Reflect on the total sum of who you are and all the meaningful contributions (big or small) you're making to your family on a regular basis. You mean so much to others, *especially* to your kids. I highly doubt they would describe you as a failure. If your kids have the basics – if they are cared for, fed, loved, safe, and alive – I want to hug you and honor you for that. Providing those things is a full-time job in and of itself.

My response to my kids that day in the car when we were returning from the beach was simply, "It's not too late." It's not too late to learn to play the piano. It's not too late to play the violin or basketball or to learn to speak Spanish. It's not too late to find and pursue your own hobbies, interests, and passions. My husband and I did the best we could with what we knew at the time, based on who we were and what we were balancing. And because I wholeheartedly believe that, guilt trips are not welcomed here anymore. One day, all our kids will get to create a life for themselves. They can build on the opportunities we gave them, or lament over the ones they missed. We all get to choose. Our kids are ours to love, care for, shape, steward, and raise for only a short time. Though not perfectly, I've done just that.

To learn more about overcoming "mom guilt" and becoming more mom confident, click here for a free video resource: www.mirellaacebo.com/free

Chapter 3

SOS for the Overwhelmed MOM -
Mrs. Noah

(Genesis 6-8)

Our family takes an annual fishing trip to the beautiful eastern Sierras each summer. It's what my husband did as a kid and it's what we do with our kids. June Lake is one of our favorite spots, known as the "Switzerland of California." It's a picturesque resort community with stunning views and trout-filled lakes. We always stay in a small cabin across the street from the water. I insist on a cabin – any cabin – because I like my basic creature comforts: a kitchen, a toilet, a bed and four walls. I'm spoiled that way. The cabins are fully furnished and have just about everything we need to call them home for a week – including a stack of cork tokens on the kitchen counter that translate to free coffee from the local restaurant on property. Score!

I like to print my packing list and prepare for our trip several weeks in advance. My goal is to avoid the overwhelm that always strikes at the 11th hour. I'm sure you know what I'm talking about – it's when the mom brain goes into overdrive and starts preparing for all the "what ifs" and "just in cases." It's when you rehearse every possible scenario in your head, every mishap, every possible emergency too. "Did I pack A or B just in case X or Y happens?" It's Overwhelm Central. Too many open brain tabs with no chance at closing them until we start to drive toward the mountains. If this is what happens to prepare for vacation in a small family of four *without* pets in tow, I can't imagine what it'd be like bringing them, too. No thanks.

I start with this small example of overwhelm to help us distinguish between productive overwhelm and not-so productive overwhelm. In the case of packing for a family vacation, the feeling of overwhelm is hopefully short-lived but productive. It serves a purpose, since we're required to double down on our efforts *now* in exchange for the carefree vacation that's coming. However, this was hardly the case for the brave and likely overwhelmed Mrs. Noah, who, at God's command, willingly packed up her things, her family, and a whole zoo of animals for a life-changing ark adventure.

Scripture doesn't tell us much about the unnamed woman behind the monumental flood story, but what we do know is that behind every good man, there's a good woman helping to make things happen. Who was she, and what can we learn from her?

Before I continue, here's my disclaimer. Because Scripture is silent about Noah's wife and her role as a mom and wife, I've taken some liberties in my descriptions. Everything I'm about to share is speculation and my opinion; I'm no scholar. I'm a curious mom who loves God, as well as a life coach with lots of questions. Thus, I take the space here to offer those two perspectives. Now, back to the story.

It's reasonable to think Mrs. Noah was a woman of strong faith who supported her husband. It's reasonable to think she played an active role in helping him with the ark while raising their three boys. And it's also reasonable to think at some point, she was overwhelmed by all of it. God had called them to the biggest assignment of their life: He wanted them to build a boat, fill it with animals, endure a worldwide flood, and then start anew. As much as I love my husband, I'd be asking God for the burning bush to speak to me on this one. The boat plan was nuts, especially since it had never rained up until that point and there was no human concept of a flood. Even the most faith-filled among us would likely think twice.

Was Mrs. Noah overwhelmed by this God-sized plan He had for her life? After all, what they were about to do would not just affect her life, but the life of her entire family as well as the rest of the world! Honestly, I think anytime God asks us to do anything, it feels big and overwhelming. But this was *really* big, and I'm sure it felt *really* overwhelming. Just imagine for a moment the blueprint for construction of the massive ark alone. This wasn't just a kitchen makeover. This was a major project of overwhelming proportions, which took about 100 years to complete. There was so much to do, plan, build, organize, and endure, *including* the public mockery as the couple forged ahead in full sight of the hostile world around them. If they lived in the day of social media, they'd be shredded. Remember, no one else believed Noah's crazy tale... except his family. The idea that God would destroy the world? Why? What kind of God does that?

Scripture says the earth was so corrupt and full of violence that God wanted to put an end to it, and the fact that Noah didn't protest tells me he agreed. God knew nothing good would come from a world like that, so He acted in justice and in mercy. He judged evil by wiping it out and showed mercy by sparing anyone who believed and got into the boat. God destroyed evil with His flood, as well as the pain and suffering that goes with it. He also entrusted the future of humanity to a family of eight: the Noahs. God doesn't play. He doesn't allow willful sin to continue indefinitely; eventually, He will bring consequences to the world. This may seem mean, but it's quite the contrary. God does this because He's merciful, and he doesn't want us to get so far removed from Him that we can't find our way back.

I'm guessing that in her own life of raising children and teaming up with her husband, Mrs. Noah wore many of the same "hats" we moms wear today. Whether we're managing a household on an ark or on land, mom life is mom life. Our daily chores and responsibilities are similar, and they don't stop. Mrs. Noah was likely in charge of cooking, cleaning, caretaking, and tending to and feeding the animals. I have four small pets who are domesticated, but they're darn messy – adorable – but still messy. Cleaning two litter boxes every day has me questioning their cuteness. How did a busy Mrs. Noah do it all? How did she keep it together day in and day out? Was she physically, mentally, emotionally, and spiritually drained from the daily grind, just like we can become? Her family spent about a year inside that boat. I can't even imagine that. Oh wait... yes I can. The Covid-19 lockdown gave us all a little taste of that isolating feeling, and it was, to say the least, no bueno. Just like we felt overwhelmed by all the uncertainty of what life would be like on the other side of the pandemic, I think Mrs. Noah probably felt some of that too. She spent quite a long season at sea with her family. Even on the best cruise line, my max away from dry land is seven days. Period. And that's with fancy meals, live shows, and a waterslide.

What can we learn from Mrs. Noah? What would she say to today's overwhelmed mom? Perhaps she would simply tell us she took it one day at a time, one task at a time, with her eyes fixed on God the entire time. The truth is, whatever God calls us to do, He will equip us for. Just like God gave Noah specific instructions on how to build the ark and the skills with which to do it, I believe He gave Mrs. Noah the wisdom, strength, and perseverance she needed to do her part. I believe He gives us everything we need to make it through, too.

Maybe you're a working mom, a stay-at-home mom, a single mom, or a mom who's caring for your mom – and you're overwhelmed. Maybe you're a mom who heads the PTA, or you volunteer, or you're involved in ministry, service, or leadership – and you're overwhelmed. Moms, before we continue, I'm gonna ask you to sit up straight, chin up, close your eyes, take a deep breath, put your hand on your heart, and show yourself some love and care. Take a moment to acknowledge your hard work. Honor your hard work, sacrifice and strength, and allow yourself to feel some gratitude for what you *are* doing well, instead of what you aren't. Give yourself this daily gift.

I recently did a workshop where I walked participants through a brain map activity. For my visual learners out there, essentially it was a way to *see* their "overwhelm" at a glance. You can do this exercise too, at any time and using any word you'd like in order to deconstruct and better understand the concept. In this case, I asked the participants to write the word *overwhelm* in the middle of a blank piece of paper. Then, I asked them to do a brain dump, writing down everything they associated with that word, including everything that puts them in that state. I invite you to try it. My "overwhelm" brain map included phrases like: "news," "current events," "social media threads," "my to-do list," "the meeting I'm not prepared for," "my overactive thought life," and "weighty decisions I need to make," just to name a few. I asked everyone to get as specific as possible. I asked them what being in a state of overwhelm looked and felt like, as well as who they became when they were in it. How was it holding them back? What was it keeping them from doing, being, or experiencing? If you struggle with constant overwhelm, it's undoubtedly keeping you from something else that is meant for you.

When I'm overwhelmed, I'm moody, short, scattered, and impatient. It's hard for me to be fully present. When I'm in this state, I also blame and complain more than I care to admit. All in all, I'm not exactly a "fun time." This stinks, because I actually *want* to be. I *want* to enjoy my life. I *want* to enjoy my kids and appreciate the small things. I *want* to be grateful and content. I *want* to be patient and peaceful. And overall, I *want* to live a balanced life. Essentially, the last six sentences are what my overwhelm keeps me *from*. Yikes. So, what can I do? What am I *willing* to do – if anything at all?

For starters, let's return back to the first brain map and examine the things that cause overwhelm. Ask yourself: Where do I have the power to change some things? What do I need to let go of in order to have more space for God to work in my life? It might be something tangible, like an event or activity on your busy calendar. However, it could go deeper than that. It might be something like control, worry, fear of not having enough or being enough. Imagine the freedom that awaits once you can let go of some of those things. Sometimes, less really is more – more sensible, more fulfilling, more engaging. Maybe Jesus is asking you to give something up so you have time to deepen your relationship with Him. When we make God our top priority, He helps us order our life in a way that brings calm, not chaos.

So what's causing your overwhelm? Is it something that's in your control or outside of your control? If you're not sure, humor me for a second and close your eyes. Picture yourself sitting inside your proverbial ark of protection, a place where you feel safe and sound and grounded. Open your eyes and look around for a bit. Don't rush. Yes, you may have lots going on and lots to do inside, but everything is familiar - the mess, the chores and the many errands. You recognize these things as things you're fully responsible for and likely feel some level of satisfaction when you complete. Think of these things as what you can affect and/or change. Next, picture the things that are *outside* of your proverbial ark – the stuff you can't really change, from big headline news and current events to when your child gets sick or the price of groceries increases. I guarantee that if you're spending more time thinking about the things outside of your ark – the things you can't control – you have a fast pass to feeling overwhelmed. Whatever you're constantly thinking about is what you'll absorb.

If you like to journal, I would suggest spending some quality time meditating on this. See what God shows you. I also suggest using the Serenity Prayer as a guide. The prayer is this:

"God, grant me the serenity to accept the things I cannot change, courage to change the things I can, and wisdom to know the difference."

The key words in this prayer are *acceptance, courage, and wisdom*. We need all three, don't we, moms? I presume Mrs. Noah did too, every single day on that ark. Hers was not an easy life, and neither is ours.

Since the fall of man in Genesis, life has been hard. Why do we expect anything different? When Adam and Eve broke fellowship with God in the garden, they also broke fellowship with each other. From that point forward, life has been hard. Relationships are hard. Work is hard. Juggling kids is hard. Raising kids is hard. Maintaining a household is hard. Paying bills, caring for our parents, honoring commitments – all of it is hard. And overwhelming.

So, what do we do? Do we resign ourselves to a hard life that leaves us feeling overwhelmed? The short answer is: No. In many ways, the flood story is dreadful and sad, but it's also one of great hope and incredible promise. It reminds us that God comes to our rescue. He saves us and gives us rest from what surrounds us. God doesn't want us living in a constant state of overwhelm. He is Emmanuel, God with us, and He wants to walk with us through life. He wants us to bring the things that overwhelm us to Him. He wants a relationship so intimate and personal that every day, we seek His help. It doesn't matter if our requests are big or small – what good parent doesn't want to help their child? If you're a Believer then you're His child, and with that comes the privilege of knowing and being known by your Maker. As we ask for His help and yield to His spirit, He rescues us daily from ourselves, our ways of thinking, our attitudes, and yes, our overwhelm. He gives us a heavenly perspective and a peace that surpasses all understanding.

In all of this, we have a choice to make. Do we drown in the overwhelm or get into the ark? The ark resembles Christ. Mrs. Noah didn't die in the flood because she was safe in the ark. If you're in Christ, you too are in a place of safety. Those who enter are safe. God equips us for the everyday and wants to speak to us in the depths of our overwhelm. He wants to help bring order and peace to our daily lives, but we have to take the first step by prioritizing Him. Speaking to Him first. Do you make room for God to speak to you daily? Do you make time to connect with Him personally so He can renew your thoughts and mind, increase your strength, and build you up? On our own, we can easily feel inadequate to face what's hard and overwhelming. We have to seek Him first.

I believe this is what Mrs. Noah did. I imagine she recognized how much she needed the Lord every day – every hour of every day, on the good days and the hard days. I imagine she depended on Him greatly and learned to trust him more and more with each passing day. I imagine God was changing her through her overwhelming circumstances and responsibilities, and that over time, her faith was strengthened. She endured so much and continued to persevere, and I can't help but think she was a different person by the time she stepped off the ark. God was training her up and preparing her for her next season, and He's doing the same with us.

God knows all that's on your plate today and He wants to help you with it. How can you let him in? Start your day with meditation and prayer. Start with setting aside your daily agenda, your own ideas, your overactive thoughts, and any concerns or distractions you have. Take a minute to be still and breathe. Close your eyes, open your hands – palms up, as a sign of your willingness to receive what He has for you. Picture His grace overflowing into every part of your day. Allow yourself to feel His presence and let God speak directly to your heart. Ask Him: How do You want to use me today? What are You asking me to release today? What do I need to clear out of my life so I have more space to hear Your voice?

Every day for almost a year, Mrs. Noah must've worked hard to forge ahead with her daily tasks aboard the ark. She likely went to bed exhausted, only to get up the next day and become exhausted all over again. Most of us can relate to the monotony of our everyday routine. Most of us can probably also relate to that feeling you get when you think you've figured things out, and then God asks you to take on more. Really God??? "I'm already busy enough and you want me to do MORE?!" It's happened to me, and maybe it's happened to you too.

For years, I was asked to volunteer either at school, church, or various mom groups. No thanks. "My kids *are* my ministry," I'd say. I was proud of myself for that answer because it got me out of having to do a bunch of other things. That worked for a while, until one day I was struck by this thought: What if by always saying no, I was missing out on something God had planned for me? What if God was actually inviting me to take on *more*? Crazy, right? All I knew to say for years was "no thank you," until I realized all of these instances could have actually been missed opportunities to let go of what *I* wanted so I could grow into what *He* wanted for me. With some hesitation, I started saying yes to things – yes to working in Sunday school, yes to leading Mommy and Me, yes to teaching at Vacation Bible School, yes to leading a small group, then a big group, then teaching on a small stage, then a large stage. I'm sharing all this not to brag but to tell you that truthfully, the more I've said "yes" to God, the more God has grown me up.

Leadership has helped me discover my gifts, learn new skills, contribute beyond myself (and family), and use everything I possess for God's purposes. I've learned to see my value and worth outside of motherhood. I'd like to think I've become a better mom, wife, and human being too. God has helped me grow my identity in Him and find a much bigger purpose than I previously thought was possible for myself. He taught me that being in a state of overwhelm was really an invitation to recalibrate, reprioritize, set some boundaries, and ultimately, let go of some things and *let God* lead the way.

So, is the moral of my story that if you're feeling overwhelmed, you should perhaps take on more?! This isn't always the case, but for me, it was just what I needed. Once I got real clear on what was most important in my life, I learned to be okay with releasing some of the less necessary things on my plate – even if they were "good" things. All things seem important, but not all things are of equal importance. I learned to delegate and let others (e.g., my kids) be responsible for their own things. I learned to trust more and control less. I learned to discipline my thought life and not worry as much.

Moms, we have a moral responsibility to be an example to our kids in all areas of life, including how we deal with overwhelm. They're learning how to deal with life by watching us. Whatever we say and do when we're overwhelmed, whatever that looks like, they're seeing it and will likely mirror it. If our tendency is to get flustered, blame, complain, shrink back, lash out, or whatever else, we are missing out on teachable moments. Life will be hard. We'll be overwhelmed sometimes. Whatever God's teaching you in your time of overwhelm is a great lesson to pass on to your kids.

I believe God has a calling on my life and your life – just like he had for Mrs. Noah's life. I believe the moment she embraced her calling and chose to faithfully walk with the Lord through the unknown, God gave her the courage and strength to endure her daily life on the ark. What a strong and powerful witness she must've been for her three daughters-in-law who were also in the boat. No doubt her daily example impacted them for the rest of their lives, just like our actions and reactions can impact our kids for the rest of theirs.

I'll leave you with a final thought. I imagine Mrs. Noah was like us and had friends and other people in her life she cared about. My guess is they weren't women of faith, because none of them got into the boat. It's hard to be a light in a dark world. I imagine it was as hard back then as it is today. That's why community and church family is such a gift! We ought to be surrounding ourselves with likeminded people and friends who are walking in faith. Real joy is being with Jesus and the people who love him. Find your tribe, your spiritual family. Find the people of faith who will get into the boat with you – people who will remind you of *who* you are and *whose* you are. Those who share your vision and values and who will bring you back to Christ when you need it the most.

When my kids were little, I joined everything that came my way: MOPS, Mommy and Me, Mom's the Word, small groups, school groups, and Bible Study Fellowship. The women and moms in these groups were my lifeline. We shared our lives and lived our stories together – our highs and lows, struggles, failures, and doubts. Being able to have real conversations with other new moms helped me feel normal, validated, and less alone in my feelings of overwhelm, because I knew other moms were going through similar challenges, too. We could relate to each other. The beautiful thing is, I discovered it was a two-way street. As much as I gleaned from the older and wiser moms, it turns out I also had wisdom to share that was valuable to others. The more I shared, the stronger and more confident I felt. It's a beautiful thing to encourage and be encouraged. It's why I encourage moms to find an older and wiser mom who's further along in her journey *as well as* a younger mom who's right behind them. Both are of great value. There's power in connection, meaningful relationships, deep sharing, storytelling and interaction. All of it is a game changer.

God loves you and wants to be with you in your overwhelming moments. He wants you to share with Him what's on your mind. Always remember to pray it out. When you're overwhelmed and in doubt, pray it out. God may not remove the overwhelming circumstances from your life. Instead, He may very well want to grow you through what you go through.

Chapter 4

SOS *for the* Impatient MOM - *Sarah*

(Genesis 12, 16)

I like to think I'm a good mother, but sometimes, I'm impatient. I yell. I've said things and thrown things out of frustration. I've done things I'm not proud of. Have you?

In my experience, an impatient mom can be a scary mom. It's hard to keep your composure when you're made to wait for something you want *right now,* especially when it involves your family. Am I right, moms? When our kids are young we need patience as they grow, develop, and reach those important milestones like walking, talking, eating, and dressing themselves. We need patience again as they learn to read and write, or when they try to tell us their long-winded story of what happened at school that day. And we need even *greater* patience when our kids start taking on household chores and we're waiting for them to throw out the trash, unload the dishwasher or walk the dog

- the *first* time they're told! Sometimes we're waiting for our husbands to clean the garage so we have a direct route to the washer and dryer. Now, I'm not saying I'm describing my own life but hey... if the shoe fits Cinderella!

Life is good – really good – at exercising our muscle of patience. Our everyday circumstances outside of the home also have a way of teaching us to wait for things. We wait in traffic, at restaurants, coffee shops or carpool pick-up after school. And how about when you're waiting in the check-out line at the grocery store behind the customer with the 32 coupons. Oh, the joys of that! (Though, I'm truly happy for their savings.)

One of my personal favorites is having to wait during the third trimester of pregnancy while you're waddling around, everything hurts, and you feel like dying. (That was me with both kids.) Or when an author goes on and on and on to make her many points. Any way you slice it, waiting is hard. Maybe that's why patience is a virtue... because sometimes, it hardly seems attainable.

Let's talk about Sarah, Abraham's wife in the book of Genesis. In the Bible, Sarah is the woman who waited and waited and waited. She waited a whopping *25 years* for God to make good on a promise He'd made her. That's a heck of a long time! And though we can clearly see her dedication and faith "in the waiting," we can see her flaws, too. Let's dig deeper into her story and discover what we can learn from her.

Once upon a time, God decided to choose a group of people, set them apart and start the nation of Israel. Why? God's plan was to reveal Himself to them so they in turn could reveal God to the world. This was their specific purpose. When you think about it, that's some high expectations! God showed His favor on this young nation and began a personal relationship with them so the world could see what an intimate relationship with God looks like. Of all the people in the world God could have picked to begin the nation of Israel, God chose Abraham and Sarah - a wrinkled, old couple without kids. What an interesting choice.

Following God's instructions, the pair stepped out in faith and into the unknown. They left their family, as well as their home, and went to a place they knew nothing about. It was a brave move on their part and it showed immense faith. God promised this couple He'd turn them into a great nation someday, and that Sarah would be the matriarch of nations and kings alike. Abraham and Sarah would have as many kids as there were stars in the sky, God had said. But... wait. Let's hit the brakes for a second. How? And when? Sarah and her hubby were senior citizens when this all started; her biological clock had most definitely stopped ticking. Mood swings, hot flashes, even menopause were likely all things of the past for her at this point. Sarah didn't know *how* or *when* God's promise would be fulfilled, but she believed it would, and she waited. Year after year, but for so long, nothing. As mentioned before, it would take two and a half decades for God to give her a miracle baby. Yes, baby Isaac did arrive... eventually. The problem was this: Ten years after God made his original promise – a decade into waiting for a baby of her own but 15 years before she would get one – Sarah had grown *impatient*, and I can't say I blame her. She made things happen the only way she knew how. A lousy practice by today's standards, Sarah had Abraham sleep with her handmaid, Hagar, as was customary in their time. Hagar conceived Ishmael, and it's a good thing God knows all already, because there's no way they could have explained themselves out of that one.

So yes, Sarah did wait. She did bear a son... in time. In God's time. However, she also rushed ahead of His plan. She went into what some moms might call "fix-it" mode. Her impatience built up over years of waiting, causing her to take matters into her own hands.

Ever been there – in a place where your impatience reaches a tipping point and you can no longer keep waiting? A place where you cross over with frustration into "nevermind-I'll-just-do-it-myself" mode? I think that's all of us from time to time, because waiting is hard and we are naturally impatient. So what does that really make us? Hmm. I would say this makes us perfectly impatient.

What do you think? Was Sarah patient or impatient? Is it possible to be both at the same time? Honestly, I think Sarah gets a bad wrap. It's so easy to point out the faults in other people while completely neglecting our own. I don't fault Sarah for doing what she did; being childless in that society brought a lot of cultural shame and the surrogate mother strategy was common practice. Plus, in my opinion, she had already waited a really long time for God to make good on His word. I'm sure she longed for her baby to come – a baby she could love, hold, and raise as her own. Her heart must've grown with anticipation and eagerness with each passing year, only to be disappointed time and time again. I wonder if Sarah began to doubt whether she would ever be a mom. Did she wonder if she had misunderstood God's plan for her life? How regularly did she remind herself of God's promise to her and Abraham?

"'I will make you into a great nation, and I will bless you; I will make your name great, and you will be a blessing.' (Genesis 12:2). He later promised: "I will make your offspring like the dust of the earth, so that if anyone could count the dust, then your offspring could be counted." (Genesis 13:16)

Ultimately, Sarah did become a mom. She was 90 years old, Abraham was 100. Why did God make this family wait so long? Honestly, it seems cruel on the surface. Did God forget about what He had said? Did He change His mind? Was it a test?

God doesn't forget His promises, nor does He change His mind. God's promise to Sarah actually *required* her to wait. Let that sink in for a moment. Sarah's faith needed to grow in order to prepare her to be the mother she needed to be for Isaac. Isaac's birth required God's miraculous intervention in <u>His</u> timing, not hers, so no one else could take credit.

I honestly think one of the hardest things for us moms to do is to wait. We *want* to be patient, I know we do. But how often do we jump into a situation in order to run interference, trying to fix things on our own? How often do we run ahead of God in a season of waiting? It got me thinking. Perhaps being a "patient mom" has less to do with how long we wait for something and more with who we're *being* and *becoming* while we're waiting. Does this resonate with you? This resonates with me for sure. But no matter how much I believe this to be true, I'm still impatient. So this story causes me to think: What can we learn about God and the Sarah in all of us?

<u>First, God</u>: God always keeps His promises. He's a God who *is* who He says He *is* and *can do* what He says He *can do*. If God makes a promise, He keeps that promise. He keeps His word. We can trust Him. God doesn't change His mind and He doesn't forget His people. He gave Sarah His word; and what He said would happen actually *did* happen. Granted, God's plan unfolded slowly, but it unfolded nonetheless. God isn't in the same hurry that we are. He is outside of time and space, and His timing isn't our timing. If it seems like God is distant, removed, or has forgotten you, He isn't. He hasn't. He's just not in the same kind of rush that we are. Waiting is always for our good and our growth. God shapes us in the waiting. He wants

us to trust Him in the waiting. He wants us to watch with anticipation and be on the lookout for unexpected answers.

Next, Sarah (the real person and the little bit of her that lives in all of us): Sarah believed God even though sometimes she struggled to believe God. Can you relate? Do you ever doubt, question, or struggle believing that God is real and His word is true? Difficulty believing is a very natural response, if you ask me. God is invisible and infinite and we're physical and finite. Our minds cannot fully comprehend a God we cannot see, feel, or touch. We know just enough, but not enough. We have *some* of the puzzle pieces but we don't always know how they fit together. Sometimes we wonder if they can even fit together at all! We all have a Sarah inside of us, and I want to encourage her. Whatever you're waiting on the Lord to do for you right now, continue to seek Him wholeheartedly. Keep your eyes focused on God's character and promises. Those two things are unchanging. When we take our eyes off of God and focus solely on our situation, that's when we're tempted to take matters into our own hands. That's when we want to take control. I want to encourage you to have an action plan when you're in a season of waiting. What attributes of God can you remind yourself of, what promises can you stand on? Sarah may have "failed" to trust God completely, but God didn't fail her. He followed through. He delivered. And this is true in our lives, too. God sees us and still loves us, even when we "fail" to wait for Him.

Why do you think waiting on God is so difficult? Pause and think about that for a moment. I think there's lots of answers to this question, but I'll hone in on one. Simply put, waiting on God requires faith. I'll add, it requires a level of faith none of us have yet. Boom. I said it. That's a truth bomb worthy of some deep reflection. The truth is, none of us has perfect faith. No one person is nailing it all the time, every single day. Just like we grow tired and impatient with our kids, spouse, relationships, and all other areas in life, we can also grow tired and impatient in faith. I've learned this about myself in my own journey and it's not anything I feel shameful about. You shouldn't, either.

Okay, I've said it several times already: Waiting is hard, and it doesn't come to us naturally. We want what we want, when we want it. So, what should we do when we're in a season of waiting and it *feels* impossible?

Answer: Activate a level of faith *greater* than what we currently have. That's a loaded statement, and it's worth unpacking. First, what is *faith*? More specifically, what does *faith in God* look like? Let's start with this basic distinction: Believing in God <u>isn't</u> the same as faith in God. A belief system is more about head knowledge – a.k.a., knowing facts about God (He is loving, holy and good; the Creator and Sustainer of all things etc.). Faith *in* God is an action – it's acting *as if* you believe those things are true. In other words, it's acting in agreement with who He says He is and giving God the benefit of the doubt in our season of waiting - *especially* when we don't understand it all. That's how we activate faith. It's saying, "Because I believe You are who You say you are, I am *choosing* to trust you (with my life circumstance) because maybe - just maybe - there's something I'm not seeing that You do. Maybe there's something you want to show me, teach me? Maybe this is somehow for my good and my growth?"

We've all been given a measure of faith. Each one of us. And we're placing our faith somewhere, in something or in someone. Some of us are placing our faith solely in ourselves, and as a result, we're left with relying purely on ourselves. We believe we're in control, we know what's best and if we don't act, everything will fall apart. That's a pretty big burden to carry, and it comes with a lot of demands, anxiety and worry. Where else are we placing our faith? We tend to put our faith in things that bring us security, like our careers, money, and relationships, to name a few. However, faith in God maintains the belief that He is large and in charge, and above all of those things. The truth is we don't come to faith in God on our own; God opens hearts and unlocks minds so we can understand what we otherwise can't understand, apart from His help. He shows us how we're not really in control of all the things we think we are. Life requires faith. This is why Scripture says we walk by faith and not by sight. God is always asking us to trust Him with something, which likely means He's asking us to wait on something too. Faith in God, and trusting Him, isn't a blind leap; it's based on who He is. Who is God to you?

There's a meme I came across recently that pretty much sums up the Christian life as a life of waiting. "Joseph waited 13 years, Abraham waited 25, Moses waited 40, Jesus waited 30... If God is making you wait, you're in good company." It took me a minute before it clicked, but in a sense, it's true. The Old Testament is full of stories of people waiting for a Savior. The New Testament is full of people waiting for Jesus's return - which includes us. Until then, we get to try our hand at being patient. However, we don't need to stay idle while we wait. Instead, we're called to conform to the image of Christ in our waiting. That's our assignment, but it consists of more than enough to keep us busy forever. Are you trying to look more like Jesus in your times of waiting? I believe that's the only way we can know that we're doing it right.

Let's circle back to patience in motherhood. As I've said before, no matter what age or stage our kids are in, we need lots of patience with them. I recall a mom sharing with me how impatient she was when teaching her son how to read. He'd hold the oversized book in his hands, and with laser focus and great amounts of effort, he would slowly sound out the letters, "R-RE-RE..." but before he could finish, "It's 'RED,'" the mom would blurt out, "The word is 'red!'" Next word, "B-BL-BLA..." "It's 'BLACK.' The color is 'black!'" I still think about her every so often, and every time I nod in agreement. Yep, that was me, too.

Because patience requires practice *and* an action plan, here's a list of ten basic TIPS to help you grow in patience no matter your child's age:

1. Slow down and be still. It's hard to be patient when you're in a constant hurry.
2. Be mindful of the things that cause impatience. Know your triggers and make adjustments.
3. Pause and take deep breaths. Inhale patience and exhale impatience. Release all the tension you're undoubtedly holding.
4. Acknowledge areas where you may need to release control. Ask God to help you.
5. Take a moment to shift your attention toward God. Ask God to help you see your situation from His perspective. What's His purpose for you in the waiting?
6. Have an action plan. Don't stay stagnant while you wait. What else can you choose to focus on?
7. Resist giving in to your emotions. What God says is true about you is more true than what your circumstances and emotions might be telling you.
8. Stay calm so you can evaluate situations objectively.
9. Practice patience. Make yourself wait by choosing the longer line at the grocery store or gas station; sometimes, pick the longer lane in traffic. Allow yourself to sit in the waiting. Find peace in it.

10. The Lord is our Sabbath rest. Join Him in that rest on a daily basis, not just once a week.

As moms, we have it in our heads that we must go-go-go all the time. Fortunately, this is not what God calls us to do. Think about the people we become in our impatience – we lash out, say mean things, and react impulsively. We get annoyed, feel angry and irritable. Impatience doesn't feel good or sit well in the body, does it? More than that, we don't tend to make good decisions when we're in this place. Then there's the fact that our kids are always watching us. What are they believing about themselves when we're impatient with them? What are we teaching them about managing emotions?

I think God is always calling out new levels of patience from within me. I can think of two main examples, which I'll share. The first is when I broke my foot at the gym eight years ago. I was deep into cross training at the time, and fell from a rope climb. I broke my talus bone and ended up in surgery with a metal plate and five screws in my left foot. I was bed-ridden for three months. I would travel from my bed to the couch, and sometimes out to the backyard. I spent many hours lying flat on my back with my foot elevated above my heart. It would take about eight months and lots of physical therapy for my foot to heal. Along the way I wore many colorful casts, walked with crutches, used a wheelchair, and hobbled around in a velcro boot before I learned to walk again. Talk about growing patience in the waiting! I was miserable. I cried a lot and wanted to give up every other day. The hardest part was not being able to rush the healing process. It has its own timeline and I was forced to respect that. I didn't like a single second of the entire process, but I did it and in the end, it taught me great patience.

A second example is when I took care of my mom during her sunset years, right before she passed away in May of 2005. She had a really long health journey that crowned me with patience. My mom had many struggles, including diabetes and Parkinson's disease. She was in and out of hospitals for different surgeries over the course of several years before she passed. My kids were little at the time; I was stretched for sure and always short on energy. Back then, it felt like all of the doctor visits, evaluations, and follow-ups were testing my patience, but now I see that they were actually building it. When you're caring for a loved one with a long list of medical issues, you need a lot of patience because nothing happens quickly. You're always waiting for tests, surgeries, medication, results, and more generally, for things to get better. Sometimes they do and sometimes they don't. In the end, I got to watch my mom handle her health journey as gracefully and patiently as she could. She was a pillar of silent strength. I truly can't believe it when I stop and think about all she endured.

As for Sarah? God had a different timeline in mind than she imagined when He promised to start a new nation through her. From His point of view, which is always a great place to start, He was putting into motion the biggest rescue plan of all time. He was in the process of saving the world through Jesus (who would come much later and through Sarah's lineage). God had the entire vision for His salvation story – beginning, middle, and end – in mind when He intentionally chose Sarah to be the matriarch of the nation of Israel. God chose her to be a *supporting* character in a long string of supporting characters, who all eventually point to the main character Christ Jesus.

The truth is, this life isn't all about us. Our individual lives are a collection of smaller stories that play a part in God's bigger story - a story that calls us to God-sized patience. I'll admit, I often lack the patience needed in my daily life but I know where to find it. In God Himself. And man, has He got patience! He's been raising children His whole life, putting up with our entitled and demanding ways every day for centuries. How has God been patient with you? How can you extend the patience you receive from Him to your kids? The beautiful thing is that you don't have to manufacture patience on your own – it's a gift from God, a fruit of the Spirit.

Galatians 5:22-23 says, "But the fruit of the Spirit is love, joy, peace, patience..." Wait... ding-ding-ding, let's stop right there. Patience? Yes, patience is the fourth fruit on the list of nine that He produces within us (the remaining five are kindness, goodness, faithfulness, gentleness, and self-control). What this means is that if you really want to grow in patience, it's yours for the taking. You just have to get out of His way. God is the one who grows our patience in those sacred, internal places of our hearts. He's our SOS when it comes to truly changing us from the inside out. You may not think it's possible, but it is. Remember, He brings new life to every area of our existence. We have the ability to take off our old nature, as Scripture says, and put on the new. You don't have to remain in your old ways or be defeated by your impatient impulses; you have the ability to *control* your impatience, rather than be dominated by it. This is so encouraging!

The beauty of this story is that God can use even our imperfect and impatient faith to accomplish good things. He can change us in our times of waiting and make us more like Jesus – if we let Him. As one quote puts it, "It takes years to grow an oak tree and weeks to grow a squash. Which do you want to be?"

Chapter 5

SOS for the Single MOM - *Hagar*

(Genesis 16 & 21)

I grew up in the 80s as a latchkey kid in the San Fernando Valley. I'm an only child who has never met my dad. And though I'm not a single mom, I was raised by one, and I have a lot to say on the matter. Let's begin.

At first glance, it would seem as though the cards were stacked against me. I was born to a single mom who came to the United States as an illegal immigrant with only a sixth-grade education. My mom was born and raised on a remote ranch in Durango, Mexico, with her eight siblings. That kind of upbringing doesn't allow for much opportunity for higher education. My mom's family farm was so remote that it was an ideal rest stop for long commuters traveling through the mountains. Her modest ranch home became a lodging place for many passers-by looking to spend the night on their way to the U.S. – the land of opportunity. Those people would eventually inspire her to leave her family and travel the same path. She came alone and was illegal until becoming a U.S. citizen in the late 1980s. That day made her so happy; she proudly recited the pledge in her broken English and waved the flag with countless others.

For years, my mom worked many minimum wage jobs. She was a housekeeper, a nanny, a seamstress, and worked in catering, until she eventually ended up on the assembly line at an airplane manufacturing warehouse. She worked at this job for over 20 years. She liked it. She was content.

A lot can be said about contentment. Her job wasn't stimulating or prestigious. It wasn't fancy or aspirational. On the contrary, it was loud. It was mundane. And it smelled. I remember because I would go to work with her on the occasional school holiday. I'd bring my backpack and coloring books, and sit at a table near her at the factory. The workers were nice. They'd make it a point to come and talk to me and comment on my drawings. I remember one time, someone gave me a ride on a dolly. There are probably rules against that now, and fines to go with it.

For a long time I arrived at school at 6:00 am, the same time the cafeteria cooks and the school director got there. Because my mom started work at that time, she made arrangements both with my school and her job to drop me off early and get to work a little late. Both parties were gracious and agreed. I remember sometimes getting to school even earlier and the doors would be locked, so we'd sit on the steps outside and wait, enjoying the crisp morning air and the chirping birds. To this day, those are still some of my fondest memories I have with my mom.

Yes, I spent a lot of time alone. And yes, I wished I had a dad. I remember watching dads pick up their daughters at the end of the day in elementary school. They would twirl their little girls in circles when they greeted them. I wished I had that, but I didn't. And that made me sad sometimes, because that's not something moms did.

As I think back to early childhood, my life was hard. But then again, whose wasn't? No, I didn't wear trendy brands, own the latest video games, or take summer island vacations. Many of my summers were spent at home watching game shows and soaps. The Price is Right was my favorite. I'd take notes, thinking one day I'd be lucky enough to sit in the studio audience and win something. Chuck Woolery was my game show crush. He hosted Scrabble and Love Connection. As for soaps? I was hooked on *Days of Our Lives* for a while – or should I say, *Days of Their Lives*, because in many ways, the show gave me a break from my own.

Having said all of that, my mom did a wonderful job showering me with the love, attention, and security every child needs. She also knew the Lord, which made all the difference.

Here's what I want to share with you, mom. Whether you're single, divorced, separated, or were never married, if you have a heart for Jesus, that alone changes everything.

My mom's trust was always in the Lord and in His provision. It's amazing to reflect back on my formative years and realize I can't remember ever feeling crushed or burdened by the weight of our struggles. My mom was very honest about our hardships. We had serious conversations and back up plans for if X or Y happened. What if Immigration and Naturalization Service (INS) raided her work place? What if she was deported? What if her diabetes resulted in hospitalization? What if? What if? What if?

There were some hardcore scenarios to consider as a kid but I have to say, I don't ever recall living in fear. And I owe that to my mom, because she didn't live in fear. She lived by faith and I saw it. She turned every "what if" into an "even if" situation – meaning "even if X," she resolved to make it work. Her attitude during hard times was remarkable. How she faced challenges was admirable. How she showed up in life honestly didn't make sense. Looking back, I can see how the Lord really carried her and by default, carried me, too. I didn't get everything I wanted but I had everything I needed, and that was enough. I can see God's provision in the used clothes I got from my mom's coworkers and the homes we were invited to for holiday dinners, but more importantly, I can see it in the peaceful way we lived everyday. We lived paycheck to paycheck, shopped at garage sales and thrift stores, and lived in apartments my whole life. It's what I knew. Not having much in terms of material things taught me a lot of lessons that have served me well. I wasn't attached to things growing up; I learned to distinguish between what I wanted and what I *needed*. Being raised by a single mom caused me to mature pretty quickly. I had far more responsibilities than the average kid, and that was okay. In the end, I learned to work hard, be resilient, persevere, not be afraid of life, and to be content with little — these are all invaluable things that have served me well in adulthood. I've always had lots of drive and a "can do" attitude about things because I watched my mom do the same. She was sweet and soft spoken on the outside, but on the inside, she was a faith-filled warrior.

Moms, all this goes to say, what you believe matters. How you show up every day matters. How you trust the Lord matters. What you say to your kids as a single mom matters. Your kids are watching you during the hard times. What lessons are they learning from you? What example are you showing them? How is your tough circumstance shaping their view of the world, God, and themselves? My mom's hope and strength came from the Lord. Every day was a new opportunity to be grateful for what we had and to put it to good use. She always found a way. Instead of constantly worrying and projecting that worry onto me, she lived by faith. Every need we had was an opportunity to call on God for help, and this taught me that *how* we respond in the valleys of life matters.

This leads me to Hagar's story in the Bible. If you're not familiar with it, let me warn you, it's a heartbreaker. Hagar was a single mother and slave girl who was used, abused, and kicked to the curb with her teenage son, Ishmael. She was desperate to provide for her little family, but couldn't. At one point, when Ishmael was on the brink of death, Hagar sat him down in the shade of a bush and walked away. She couldn't bear to watch him die. Luckily, she didn't have to, because in the moments when all hope seemed lost, God showed up for Hagar. Twice He appeared to her in the desert, first when she was pregnant and alone, and again after she had been banished by Abraham. Both times, God reassured her that everything would be okay. There was something rather significant about Hagar's one-on-one encounters with God. We know this, because she was the only person in the Bible who gave God a name after He revealed Himself to her. The name she used translates to "You are the God who sees me." She then confirmed after His second visit: "I have now seen the One who sees me" (Genesis 16:13). That is the incredible legacy Hagar left behind. Hagar communed with the Lord in desperate times. The God of Abraham, Isaac, and Jacob revealed Himself to her, an Egyptian slave girl. God encouraged her, giving her faith to believe and eyes to see the future He had for her and her son. Her encounters with Him changed Hagar and the trajectory of her life as a single mom.

I realize, looking back at my own childhood, that Hagar's story is very much like my mom's story. My mom was pregnant and alone, unsure of how she was going to birth and raise me by herself. She considered abortion, but didn't follow through. She decided instead that she'd stop drinking and smoking for my sake, and try to be the best mom she could be, whatever that looked like. As I said before, she had an elementary school education and in some ways was childlike herself, but when it came to living by faith, she was at the top of the class. I'm still in awe of her. How did she live day to day, shouldering all the responsibility that came with raising a child by herself? How did she not shrink back and give up? Answer: She too had an encounter with "the God who saw her." It changed her life, and subsequently, it changed mine. My mom didn't simply know stuff *about* God, she *knew* God, personally and intimately. She loved God and was so confident that He would always take care of us. What's taken me decades to learn for myself through reading and studying Scripture, my mom knew naturally. She may not have been able to provide much in terms of material things, but what she did provide for me spiritually had far greater value and security.

Our homes are training centers, moms. Our homes are where God has placed us to be leaders. Every day, we're leading our kids somewhere. You and I, whether single or not, are being called to be leaders in our homes and to prepare our kids for adulthood. What we say and do in hard times is how we teach our children what to say and do when their hard days come. And oh boy, they will come. We have our kids for at least 18 years, if not more. Every day, they learn by watching us. They observe and internalize what they see us do. We're their role models and we have the God-given responsibility to show up in the way we're called. Christian mom, are you calling on the name of the Lord in your time of need? When was the last time you recalled His good promises? Which of God's many attributes will you meditate on today to encourage you? Over and over again, God proves Himself faithful to His many names. He saves, so we call Him our Savior. He comforts, so we call Him our Comforter. He helps and provides, so we call Him our Helper and Provider. He's also our refuge and strength in our time of need. He gives us rest. Of all His names, which is most meaningful to you? Which one speaks to your current need? If God has awakened your heart to faith, then you're His child and when we call on His name, it's to help us recall who He is. He's our Father in Heaven, who loves His children and never abandons them.

I didn't get to experience that kind of love and loyalty from an earthly father, and maybe you didn't either. But I'm here to tell you, that kind of fatherly love is available from God Himself. He's the Father who longs to have you and hold you, to care and provide for you. Just as we delight in giving to our kids, He delights in giving us even more. His gifts are food for the soul and spirit. He gives us strength for today, hope for tomorrow, wisdom for this afternoon's decisions, and a future that's worth it. This posture isn't easy; it requires that we come to Him like a child who wants to be loved and held. I think God loves it when we do that – when we approach Him not just as moms-in-need but as children-in-need.

Let's get back to Hagar's story. I'd like to zoom out a bit and consider the bigger historical context surrounding her life, and how that all fits into an even bigger story. Hagar's story starts with Sarah and Abraham. I covered some of the details in the last chapter, SOS for the Impatient MOM. God chose Sarah and Abraham to start the nation of Israel, even though they didn't (and couldn't) have kids. God made a crazy prediction that one day, their descendants would be as numerous as the stars in the sky. But they wondered: When? And how?

Sarah was 65 and Abraham 75 when God called them to be the people He'd use to bless the world. The years came and went, but nothing. God was silent, and Sarah grew antsy. She came up with a plan to have her husband sleep with Hagar, her slave, because that's what they did in those days. It made sense at the time. Plus, God said Sarah would have a child – maybe she thought He meant it would be through Hagar? Why not help God out a little and move the plan along? Abraham slept with Hagar and together, they had baby Ishmael. In short, Hagar was the mother to Abraham's first son because Sarah couldn't conceive. Right seed, wrong womb. The two women pretty much despised each other after that. I picture their contempt, their anger, and all the catfights in between. Maybe there was resentment because Hagar had no choice in the matter... or perhaps she bragged about being a mom and rubbed it in Sarah's face, knowing full well Sarah was barren. We don't know the emotional sources of their conflict, but it's likely both women played a part in their ongoing feud. What we do know is that the three of them – Hagar, Sarah, and Abraham – raised this little boy, Ishmael. They were there for his birth, they saw his first steps and first teeth, heard his first words, and watched him grow from toddler to teenager. It took 25 years for God to make good on his promise to Sarah and Abraham. The couple, by that point at 90 and 100, finally conceived and held their promised baby boy, Isaac – the future heir of God's people and the family line through which Jesus would eventually come.

Shortly after Isaac was born, things got worse. Whatever bad blood there was between the two moms was passed down to their boys. Sarah wasn't going to stand for it, so she insisted Hagar and her son needed to leave. This troubled Abraham. After all, he was the father of both boys and he loved them. He didn't know what to do. God reassured the distressed Abraham that both Isaac and Ishmael would be okay, so Abraham did exactly what Sarah asked. He packed up some supplies and led Hagar and Ishmael away. He sent them to the desert under God's protection, which I'm sure wasn't easy. I'm sure it was painful. Separation of the family unit is always painful.

So now what? How were she and her son going to stay alive? At one point, they ran out of water and Hagar became desperate. Ishmael was crying and she started to sob. That's the verb used in Scripture to describe what she did – sob. What a sad image. Did anyone see her suffering? Did anyone care? God saw her suffering and God did care.

"What's the matter, Hagar?" He asked. "Don't be afraid," He told her. He said to take her son by the hand. God reassured her that even though it didn't seem like it, He had a future for Ishmael, too. He insisted that one day, Ishmael would also become a great nation. Hagar may have been a slave, but this promise assured that her son and his descendants wouldn't be. That's quite a significant message. The Bible goes on to say that God was with Hagar's son as he grew up. Ishmael became a skilled archer and God basically became his dad.

Single mom, what encouragement can you receive from Hagar's story, if any? What stood out to you? I'll tell you what resonated with me: The fact that Hagar actually *sobbed* was a touching moment in my mind's eye. Hagar wasn't okay at that moment, and she didn't pretend to be. After all, Sarah had let her down. Abraham had let her down, too. To her, nothing that had happened had been okay. Sometimes, I think we pretend everything is okay when it's really not. We try hard to hide our feelings from the people around us, but God doesn't want us to hide our feelings from Him. Maybe you want to take a moment now to release whatever you're feeling inside. There's no need to keep it bottled up; it's not good for you. Give yourself time to cry if this is stirring up any heavy emotions. Tears are welcomed here. They're healing and cleansing. They're universal – even Jesus wept. Life gives us plenty of reasons to cry, and God wants us to bring our tears to Him anytime.

Maybe you need to mourn the loss of a relationship – talk to God about it. Release whatever hurts. Release the grief.

Life hurts sometimes… actually, a lot of the time. What Hagar's story teaches us, single mom, is that God rescues those with crushed spirits. He comforts the brokenhearted. He hears the desperate cries of a suffering mother. Is that you? Do you feel crushed or brokenhearted? Are you suffering right now? I invite you to close your eyes and be still, picture God wrapping His arms around you like a good Father would. If you want to cry (or sob), feel free to release it then come back to a deep slow breath. It helps regulate emotions. Now, examine your own heart. Has your release brought you closer to God, or caused you to turn away instead? Consider reaching out to a trusted person to share whatever might be coming up for you at this moment. Don't grieve alone.

After Hagar sobs, the Bible says Hagar's eyes were opened and she sees a well. A well? How did she not see that before? Is it possible she just completely missed it? After all… it's not like the well wasn't there and then it was. Or… did God make it appear out of thin air? No. Hagar didn't see it *until* she communed with God. It was after that, when He opened her eyes, that she could clearly see His provision right in front of her. What an incredible gift. We too, can commune with God and gain spiritual insight. He helps us see what we couldn't before.

Single mom, how has God provided for you? What does He want your eyes to see? God is not a distant God.

He longs for a relationship with all of us. He wants you to seek Him in your struggle – even if you doubt and question His presence. God wants to strengthen your spirit and your faith. That's your greatest need, and mine too. Yes, we have physical, financial, and health needs, but we also have spiritual needs. Your spirit likely craves rest. It needs peace. It wants reassurance. God's highest purpose for you during your hard times is for you to invite Him in. He wants you to thrive. Let Him take you by the hand and walk with you, forward. Our hope never rests on what's going on around us; it rests on Him alone.

Another thing I find incredible is that the God of Abraham personally interacted with Hagar, a common slave girl. Hagar wasn't beyond His reach. God sought her out and cared for her. This same God wants to personally interact with you, too. He wants you to have a deep encounter with Him. Hagar discovered that God sees and hears abused women. What might God want you to discover about Him during your current situation? We have to put in the effort every day to get to know Him better. Daily struggles give us plenty of opportunities to do that, don't they? Look for ways He might be speaking to you, and listen for His voice above all others. Only He can take our broken parts and hurting hearts and give us the hope and strength we need each day.

A third component of Hagar's story that stood out to me was what God said to her about her son. He told her that He had a plan for him. What a beautiful reassurance for a single mom, newly alone and figuring out what her next move should be. Hagar was likely worried about Ishmael's future and what would happen to him. If you're a single mom, it's likely you worry about that for your children, too.

Even though Ishmael was separated from his dad and he came from a broken family, God wanted to bless him. He became an archer, and a good one at that. In times of struggle, remember God also has a plan for your kids. He has gifted them with unique talents and abilities that they will discover as they grow older. Be patient, and do your best to help them discover those traits. God has a plan and purpose for every child, and He uses their exact circumstances to grow and mature them. What you're going through as a family might be central to their calling. Remember David? His brothers saw him as a lowly shepherd boy. God saw a future king. Remember Joseph and his dreams? His brothers hated him, but God turned him into a high-ranking official in Egypt. And how about Moses? He was born to a slave woman and God used him to free the Israelites after 400 years of slavery. Your circumstances don't define your kids' future. God does.

I remember going to London with my daughter's high school band several years ago. "Mind the gap" was a phrase I heard repeatedly over the intercom as we traveled by subway. It was a warning to travelers to be mindful of the distance between the platform's edge and the train. It was basically an entire foot's length of a gap (almost big enough to swallow a small child). The same applies to us and our knowledge of God. There is a huge gap between God and our limited understanding of God. We think we know way beyond our abilities, but the truth is, we know so little. There is a gigantic gap between what we see, know, and understand, and what God sees, knows, and understands. My knowledge is but a grain of sand in comparison to that of an eternal God who sees one big story. He sees our entire lives from beginning to end and knows the story He wants to tell through each person. Right now, we're simply in one of those middle chapters. There's a bigger picture that He wants to tell through the time we have here. Do you know what that picture looks like? If not, will you let Him show you?

God showed up alongside Hagar to comfort and encourage her. He told her not to fear, but to act in faith. I can testify to the fact that faith really does change the trajectory of our lives. Faith is believing God is with you and for you when things get hard. It's trusting God in the impossible moments and trusting He can do more than what we could ever possibly understand. We see life through a limited perspective and human limitations, but faith calls us to zoom out and see things with a wider perspective. Faith calls us to see things from God's perspective. God is a God without any limitations. His abilities and power far outweigh our own. Your circumstances may seem hard or even impossible for you to handle, but they're not for God. Will you trust Him?

Proverbs 3:5 says, "Trust in the Lord with all your heart and lean not on your own understanding; in all your ways submit to him, and he will make your paths straight." Another translation says it this way: "Trust God from the bottom of your heart; don't try to figure out everything on your own. Listen for God's voice in everything you do, everywhere you go; he's the one who will keep you on track." God sees your whole situation, mom. He sees your life story – beginning, middle and end. He sees your children's lives, too. Regardless of your family dynamics, you can always speak words of life over your kids. They can and will do great things. Tell them what's possible. Show them what's possible. Then, let them do what's possible.

Families were as difficult and complicated back in ancient days as they are today. Abraham had to make some hard decisions in his family, one of which was letting Ishmael and Hagar go. Abraham sought God because he needed wisdom. Moms, don't we all? We need wisdom in order to lead our families well. Most of us wish we had happy families, marriages, and kids, but sometimes, real life falls short. It can often look radically different from what we imagined. However, no matter what our family unit looks like, God is working through it. My family isn't ideal. Is yours? I struggle. Do you? Do you struggle as a single mom? Are you seeking Him daily and in every situation? The Bible is full of promises that can offer us help and hope.

As I said before, what my mom lacked in "book smarts," she made up for in wisdom. Her faith is what sustained us; I'm convinced of it. How else would someone who didn't speak English, could barely read or write, and who worked an entry-level factory job be able to raise a kid on her own in a new country? It was God's favor in our lives. It was His grace and mercy. I was (and still am) blessed without measure. I have great memories of my childhood. My mom loved the heck out of me, taught me contentment, and modeled hard work, excellence, and a strong mindset. I literally do not recall a single complaint from her of how hard we had it. She simply lived with contentment – week to week and year after year. I'm grateful for humble beginnings and for the joy and excitement I have today, as I now get to do all the things I seemingly missed out on as a kid. My mom passed away 18 years ago, but I'm still so grateful for her lasting strength that lives in me. I owe her so much.

Chapter 6

SOS *for the* Controlling MOM- *Rebekah*

(Genesis 25:19-34, 27)

Be honest: Are you a mom with controlling tendencies? Raise one hand. Do you ever try to control your kids and your husband? Raise the other hand. If both hands are raised, congrats! You've now assumed the proper posture of surrender that I believe God would want us to take each time we get the urge to control someone or something.

Someone once told me that great parenting happens when we learn to control ourselves more and our children less. Ouch. There's a truth bomb for you.

I didn't grow up in a controlling home, nor would I describe myself as being highly controlling, but I'm not gonna lie, the tendencies are there. I remember when my kids were young... If there was ever an artsy school project that needed to be done at home, it somehow became MY project. I'd start off with a suggestion here and there; by the end of the night, I'd have the perfect craft in hand and my kid was long gone. Can anybody relate?

This is clearly a benign example of what control can look like, but I point it out as proof that the tendency exists in many of us. It can show up in small ways first, but over time it becomes *the only way*. What personal examples of your own are coming to mind? Where are you insisting things be done your way, the "right" way? Simply put, we must fight the urge to control the lives of our families, moms. Fight the urge. But how? Where do we start?

When our kids are young, we step in all the time to tell them what to do and how to do it. Is this us being controlling? Not necessarily; telling and showing is appropriate for early stages of development. At some point, though, we must let go ever so slightly and enter the "let them" stage. If we've told them and shown them, it becomes time to let them.

Let them what, exactly? Well, let them make their own choices. Let them feel their own consequences. Isn't that what God did with Adam and Eve in the garden? After creating them, He taught them right from wrong and then gave them free agency to choose for themselves. God didn't force His hand or control them. He didn't run interference. He allowed them to make their own choices. Yes, He gave them the freedom to make even the "wrong" choices.

Moms, I'm not saying it's easy to extend this freedom to our kids. It's not easy, it's really hard. It's hard because our kids will undoubtedly make decisions we don't like. It's hard because we know that giving them freedom means we have less of an ability to protect them. Now, I'm not saying a mom should never intervene on her child's behalf. There are times we have to step in and overrule a decision they make but not all the time. A mother's job in her children's lives is to be just that – their mother –not a tyrant or a dictator. We don't *own our kids*. They came through us, but they're not us, and they have to discover the world through their own experiences, their own triumphs *and* failures.

In this chapter, I want to talk about Rebekah and the time her controlling tendencies were put on full display. Rebekah was a mom of twin boys, Jacob and Esau, and married to a man named Isaac (Abraham and Sarah's son). At a time when women were often submissive, Rebekah was quite strong, assertive, and decisive. I like that about her. However, what she did in this story is rather crafty and slick. She tried doing the "right thing," but went about it the wrong way. Can any mom relate?!

Before discussing the incident itself, let me give you some context and family history. It's central to why Rebekah did what she did. Like other biblical moms, Rebekah struggled with infertility – 20 years of it, to be exact. That's a really long time! Family and children were so important in those days and in their culture, so customs allowed for a man to sleep with another woman if it meant he could have a child. Yes, adultery and polygamy were the things to do. Yet, Rebekah and Isaac didn't go this route, unlike Isaac's parents (Abraham and Sarah).

Instead of having sex with another woman, Isaac prayed. Scripture says he patiently prayed for Rebekah and then waited on God. The couple waited for two whole decades! Wow, that's incredible patience.

Their prayers were finally answered and Rebekah eventually conceived, but she struggled big-time during her pregnancy. The violent jostling in her womb scared her. "Why is this happening?" she asked God. He had a prophetic answer for her, which can be found in Genesis 25:23. The Lord told Rebekah she was pregnant with twins, and that her boys would eventually separate to become two different nations. He added that the older would serve the younger and the younger would be stronger, which indicated the second born (not the first born) would be the eventual heir to Isaac's inheritance. These are all significant things to remember as we continue.

Twins Jacob and Esau grew up to be quite different from one another. Esau, the first born, was the wild, outdoorsy type. He was a hunter and very impulsive. Jacob, on the other hand, was more of a quiet homebody, a momma's boy who liked to cook. If they battled it out on a reality game show, they would be starring on Survivor vs. Master Chef. The Bible mentions Rebekah favored her younger son, Jacob, while her husband Isaac was partial to the older son, Esau. It's interesting how each parent latched onto a different son. This might be a clue into their relationship as husband and wife, and what came next as they showed more loyalty to their favorite sons than to each other.

In the couple's senior years, Isaac is blind and ready to pass on his family blessing, a.k.a. the inheritance. (Sidenote: the blessing or "birthright" of biblical times was akin to a will and testament in modern days; it included not only property and power, but also leadership of the family. Back in the day the blessing was done orally, not on paper, but was legally binding nonetheless and could not be revoked. This was a big deal!) Of course, Rebekah wanted Jacob to receive the blessing, but her husband wanted Esau, the firstborn, to have it. Isaac called Esau into his room and said that it was time to bestow the birthright, but that first, he wanted Esau to prepare a hearty meal. When Rebekah overheard this, she went into high gear and acted quickly. While Esau was out hunting, she dressed Jacob up in his brother's best clothes and had him impersonate his older brother so that he would receive the family inheritance. Rebekah cooked the meal and placed it in Jacob's hands to give to his father. Three times she told Jacob, "Do what I tell you to do," and so he did. Thanks, Mom. As questionable as her actions were, Rebekah made it happen; Jacob deceived his dad and received the family inheritance. So, what do you think? Was she right to control the situation, or should she have let her husband's desires win?

Now, I hesitate to come down too hard on Rebekah. All strong-willed and decisive moms (myself included) have our reasons for why we feel the need to step in and take charge from time to time. I mean, how else will things get done the way *we want*? It's for efficiency's sake, right?

This is just the way things are *supposed* to go, we reason as we meddle. Rebekah took matters into her own hands to orchestrate the switcheroo of her sons. Some would say she was being manipulative and deceptive; others would say she took control because she believed it's what she had to do. After all, God *did* say the older would serve the younger. Maybe in her mind, she was doing the right thing. Maybe she thought she needed to act fast to help God fulfill His promises. How many of us have tried to do something similar – impulsively intervened in a situation to force a certain outcome? Was Rebekah *really* helping God out by tricking her family?

The million dollar questions are these. Why is it so hard for us to let God be in charge? Why do we as moms often feel compelled to run the show? Why do we sometimes expend so much energy on things that shouldn't really be our concern? In other words, why can't we *let go* and *let God?* Let our children be? Let our husbands do? Sometimes we push; we prod or pull for things to work out the way we want. In the words of Janet Jackson, we believe we're in "Control." Before there was ever Beyoncé or Rihanna, there was R&B pop sensation Janet Jackson – one of my all time favorite singers in the 80s. Not to brag, but my generation had all the most iconic movies and superstars, in my not-so-humble opinion. Boy, what I wouldn't give to go back to an 80s concert. But, I digress.

So, what can we learn from Rebekah's moment of hardcore control? We can't know this for sure, but chances are, it wasn't her first (or last) display of dominance. I wonder in what other areas of life she tried to take charge. Was she controlling with her husband? If so, how did this affect their marriage? If she was more dominant, did he become passive to avoid conflict and keep the peace, or were they constantly butting heads? Whether we realize it or not, our controlling tendencies don't typically occur in a vacuum. They tend to leak into other areas of our lives and our relationships, too.

How do you know if you're a controlling mom? Let's start with defining our terms. What is *control*? *Control* in this context is preventing one thing from happening in order to make something else (the preferred thing) happen instead. Let's consider the following scenarios and questions:

- Are you constantly telling your spouse or child what to do and how to do it?

- Do you often say, "Just do as I say," or "Because I said so"?

- Are you flexible, as long as everything is exactly the way you want it to be?

- Do you ask your child to help you with something, then completely take over?

- Do you do things yourself because "no one else does it like you"?

- Do you often assume you have all the answers and the best possible outcome in mind?
- Do you assume you're right and everyone else is wrong?
- Do you tend to dominate conversations and only see things one way?
- Do you find it hard to delegate?
- Do you micro-manage tasks so things get done exactly how you want them done?
- Do you expect perfection and become distracted when things are flawed?
- Do you have a general belief that your spouse or kids are incompetent?
- Do perfection and achievement drive you?
- Do you tend to make decisions for your spouse or kids without considering what they want or need?

Let's be honest, it's just us here. Are you a few of these things or a lot of these things? More importantly, do you want to continue being these things? If the answer is, "a lot of these things" and "no," I would ask you: What kind of mom do you want to be instead? Who in your life is a great example of the mom you aspire to be? I share this list of questions not to shame or judge you; I share it to help you spot the controlling tendencies in your mom-ness and kickstart a conversation about what can be done to be better. We can't change what we don't acknowledge. If you want to control less, you must first recognize the habits and patterns you want to change.

If you identify as a controlling mom, what might be the root cause? Ask yourself, "What's behind my need to control?" Likely, it's some level and type of fear. Maybe it's fear of the unknown; oftentimes we fear a future that we see coming that we don't want or think will harm us. Could it be ego, pride, or selfishness? Sometimes we want things done our way because it brings us security in who we are. Are you someone whose mind goes directly to the worst case scenario, someone who thinks only you have the power to prevent bad things from happening? Perhaps the root cause for your desire for control is not believing a good God truly has His hand on you. Having fear is completely understandable. This life gives us a lot to be afraid of. However, remaining in fear, reacting from a place of fear, these are choices that we can decide to stop making.

My two answers to most things we want to change about ourselves are generally these: we need Jesus and we need community. Find your tribe of like-minded women who are supportive and who will hold a safe space for you to share the parts of yourself you want to change. We need good examples of godly women in our lives who have struggled or are struggling with similar things. We need accountability to stay the course. Spend more time with the women you admire and who encourage you. Talk with and glean wisdom from them. Pick women who can help you think differently, do things differently. Women who can help you see that it is in fact possible to grow and change, if you first let Jesus grow and change you.

What I like about Rebekah's story is that it zeroes in on some of our most important roles in our lives: as wives, moms, and women of faith. Let's take a deeper dive into how control might be showing up in these areas.

As WIVES – How does control show up? First, whether you've been married for one year or for 51 years, both are major milestones in my book and deserve a shout out. Anyone who's been married for over 10 minutes knows what I'm talking about. Marriage is not for the weak. It's more than floating hearts and romantic feelings; it's a serious team effort with high stakes all the time. It requires constant communication and making concessions. It asks that we routinely find ways to move toward each other, even when we're not on the same page. We learn to grow up in all the ways partnership requires: being patient and kind, extending grace and forgiveness, acting in loving ways even when we don't feel like it, owning our flaws, asking for forgiveness, and growing in character, to name a few. In other words, marriage helps us mature. We don't just grow old together, we grow up together.

Everything I just described was never modeled in my childhood. I was raised by a single mom who never married. In my early relationships, I tended to see the worst in men. I was often in self-preservation mode and held the belief that men were placeholders, impermanent. I was okay if I never got married, and more than okay if I never had kids.

The point is, I didn't learn to be a wife until I married and became one. And wow, is there a steep learning curve to becoming a good wife! I went from "independent me" to "dependent we." I became more than a singular person; I was part of a team and had to learn how to be a team player. I was responsible for taking care of "us" now, and not just in the obvious, for-better-or-worse way (although in that way, too). It became my job – as well as my husband's job – to take care of each other's innermost selves for the sake of the team. Whenever there is conflict or disagreement, I've learned to look at him as my teammate, not my enemy. I've learned that we must move *toward* each other all the freakin' time. It's not about who wins an argument, no, we can stir up so much conflict thinking like this. If he wins, then I lose. If I win, then he loses. That's a selfish win.

The real question we should be asking is, how can the *marriage* win? The marriage wins when we see it as an entity unto itself and ask, "What is good for the marriage?" rather than, "What is good for *Mirella*?" (*Insert your name there for effect.*) The marriage wins when I don't control my husband or situations we encounter together. Fighting for control doesn't help whatsoever, and it's exhausting. Over time, I've learned to keep that part of myself in check. Is this helping anyone right now?

I've learned so much in my 23+ years of marriage, so I created a marriage series on YouTube titled, "10 Things No One Told Me About Marriage." If you want to learn more about fighting fair, feeling more connected to your husband, having fun together, "winning" arguments, etc., click this link for that free video resource www.mire-llaacebo.com/free

As MOMS – How does control show up? If you're like me, you want the best for your kids all the time. You might step in, come to their rescue, and fix things for them. On the surface, these all seem like good things. But are they really? If our tendency is to take control, could we be interfering with the life lessons God wants our kids to learn? Maybe us stepping in to help is not really helping at all. How are they going to learn to interact with the world or make decisions for themselves? Advocate for themselves? How will they learn the consequences that come with their decisions? How will they learn to get back up and try again after they fall or "fail"?

Maybe part of God's plan is for our kids to face some hard stuff on their own, so they can practice walking through it. Maybe that's what will help to develop their strength, courage, grit, and resilience. Maybe that's how they will become kind, compassionate adults someday. If we're always trying to control their outcomes or keep them safe, how will they learn how to fend for themselves? I know we want to keep our kids happy and comfortable, but maybe always being happy and comfortable aren't the best life aspirations. Maybe equipping our kids with the tools for real life is a better goal, because, as we know, life requires some heavy lifting.

My daughter recently went off to college. She's my firstborn and a real doer. She takes the initiative to get things done. I really like that about her. She was accepted to college and waited for her assigned date and time to register for classes. When her day came, there were no upper level classes left. I couldn't believe it. She was only able to register for one of her 12 units; everything else was full. Wait, what? It took every ounce of deliberate intention on my part *not* to step in and fix this for her. Did I want to call the counselor, go online, check and double check the classes she wanted? Yes. Heck, I even had the idea for her to switch schools because hey, maybe it wasn't too late. Every mom's impulse inside me wanted to act, but I refrained. I gave her my suggestions and simply "let her." Remember the three stages I shared earlier? If we've *told them* and *shown them*, it's time to *let them*. It was hard, but I did it, and you can too. Here's some tips on how to do this with older kids:

- Refrain from fixing things on their behalf. Let them make their own choices.
- Ask permission to share your ideas. If they say no, respect that, otherwise anything you offer will likely be received as criticism.
- Avoid telling them what to do. If your advice is not welcomed then it is not warranted.
- Recognize that they may simply want to be heard and held, rather than fixed. (Maybe not physically

held, but emotionally held. Although, bear hugs are good too.)

- Avoid a brain dump of all your wisdom. If they're not wanting to hear you, they won't. Period.
- Be open to hearing their ideas and feedback without getting defensive.

Even the best parent in the world can benefit from these refreshers. For more ideas on how to talk to your teens, click here for another free video resource: www.mirellaacebo.com/free

As WOMEN OF FAITH -- How does control show up? Oftentimes I find myself asking God to bless my plans while I neglect to seek His. I'm so busy with the life I *want* to create, I forget about the life Jesus wants to create in and through me. When we allow God to speak to us, amazing things happen. The same God who spoke the world into existence still speaks. He gives us wisdom through His Word, His Son, His Spirit, and His people. How well are we listening? Or are we too busy controlling? Every time we're tempted to exercise control over someone or something, it's an opportunity to practice faith in full measure, beyond what's comfortable.

In Rebekah's story, who was *really* in control? Was it God, or was it the mom with the plan? Did God really need her to intervene? No, He didn't. Sometimes God will lead us to intervene in a situation and sometimes He will lead us to patiently refrain. How will you know what to do?

Surrender the moment. Surrender the control. Respond in faith. Where do you need to surrender control? Who do you need to surrender to God's perfect plans? Is it your spouse? Your kids?

Surrendering control requires that we surrender all the things behind our controlling nature: our thoughts, fears, impulses, actions, and outcomes we want to make happen. God's plans for us and our kids are so much bigger than any given moment. He sees our lives from start to finish. We can easily expend so much energy trying to control people and situations, or we can learn to rest in a good God who has ultimate control, no matter what. This distinction alone can hold our hearts steady and perhaps give us the rest we need. Which will you choose?

Chapter 7

SOS for the Lonely MOM - *Leah*

(Genesis 29-30)

Meal trains are the best! The idea of a group of friends banding together to become food fairies for a family in need is such a welcomed gift. I first heard about these at church about 20 years ago, when I was asked to donate a meal to a new mom. My cooking is not a gift to anyone, I reasoned, so I didn't sign up. Meal trains have come a long way since then. Now, there are planning tools, apps, websites, and Google spreadsheets to keep things organized so you don't end up with 10 different chicken casseroles. (No offense to the casserole.) These online planning methods also come with virtual vouchers and e-card options, which are convenient but maybe a little less memorable for the family. I'm less likely to recall who sent me the Chipotle gift card as I am to remember the friend who brought me a whole pan of baby back ribs, homemade garlic mashed potatoes, and a triple-bean mango salad with a yummy lime marinade. It was a feast from heaven's kitchen. Is it weird that my mouth still waters at the mention of marinade?

There's no doubt I love food. But, I especially love *other* people's food. I'm referring to those few friends who really love to cook and host casual gatherings. It ensures I get at least one good meal that day. I have three friends in particular who do this; they're incredible cooks and awesome hosts. They make things like homemade bread and ice cream. Plus, their charcuterie boards are what magazine covers are made of. I'm humbled when I sit at their table. Why? I must've been in the food truck line when the cooking gene made its rounds. I don't host, much less cook for the masses. I barely make enough food for my own family.

The fact that people care enough to bring you a meal is a beautiful act of service. It reminds me we don't live life in a silo. We need each other. We need a tribe of close friends, a sisterhood and community. More specifically, we need the faith and the strength of our spiritual family who will stick with us when life gets hard. These people are such a gift!

We're all hardwired for relationships. It's a basic human need to want to love and be loved by others. Another human need is to want to belong somewhere, and I would add *to someone*. We are social beings made for connection. It's what helps us feel alive. However, when we put our love in the hands and hearts of other people, it gets hard sometimes. We're not always loved in the way that we want or need. Is perfect love even possible? If so, what does it look like? And what do we do when this basic desire isn't met?

I'm reminded of the story of Leah in the Bible. If you're not familiar with her love story, it's both tragic and beautiful in a tear-jerking sort of way. Her story starts with a man named Jacob (mentioned in Chapter 6, SOS for the Controlling MOM). Jacob was running for his life from his angry brother and needed a place to hide. He ended up at his uncle's house. There, he met and fell madly in love with a girl named Rachel, his uncle's daughter. On their wedding night, and in a shocking twist, Rachel's dad swapped her out for her homely older sister, Leah. What a con job! Some would say the duped Jacob deserved it for how he duped his twin brother (over his inheritance) in an earlier story. The point is, Jacob found himself *stuck* with Leah as his wife. The Bible says he cared for her, but didn't truly love her. Jacob quickly made a deal with Leah's dad and married Rachel too, one week later. The sisters were then off to the races to see who could have the most children.

I admit, my heart breaks for Leah. It's a sad story, isn't it? She ended up a lonely married woman competing with her sister-wife for a man who didn't love her. She didn't deserve that. We don't know much about the two women, their personalities, or character. All we know is Rachel was the pretty one with the cute figure and her older sister Leah was the one with the "dull eyes" – hardly a statement any woman wants to hear. My guess is, there was something so unflattering about Leah that kept her single. Was this the only way her dad could marry her off, by conning a man? Maybe. What we do know is that Leah's shrewd dad subjected her to a marriage of long-term rejection and loneliness. The comfort here is that at some point, Leah had a God-encounter that changed her life forever. God saw Leah's suffering when no one else did and He was good to her when no one else was. Leah ultimately learned that God's love is the greatest love of all, beyond what any man could offer.

Two things stand out to me immediately about Leah's story. One is her relationship with her younger sister, Rachel, and the other is her relationship with her husband, who preferred her younger sister, Rachel, over her. Let's start with the first. I wonder what it was like for dull Leah to grow up with a beautiful younger sister. Did she feel like the ugly duckling next to her? Was Leah always second fiddle? Did she constantly judge herself and compare herself – her looks, her body, and her abilities? Do you compare yourself to other women? I think it's one of the most natural things we do, especially in the day of social media. How often do we scroll, compare, judge, and then complain about all the things we see that we're not, don't have, or aren't doing that others are, have, and are busy doing?

Moms, can I just say we have to stop being so mean to ourselves! Can we be kinder about our bodies and not complain about the wrinkles, cellulite, stretch marks, loose skin, soft arms, and added pounds? All of that is proof we've carried life. We've earned every star and stripe. Yes our bodies change after having babies, but let's not become so preoccupied with our physical imperfections that we reduce ourselves to an outer shell. As if that's all we have to offer. We have to guard our thoughts and words, or that negative talk will consume us. You're more than a physical being, mom. You're a created being with a heart, soul, and spirit. Do you spend more time criticizing your physical self than nourishing your spiritual self? Many of us spend a disproportionate amount of time beating ourselves up for our physical "flaws." We zero in on them as if that's all we are. Yes, take care of yourself, your health, and your body. That's basic common sense. But I also urge you to focus on and value the *whole you* – the entire you – and to reflect on the beautiful qualities you possess inside. These are ultimately what God values, so let's align ourselves to them.

The caution here is not to live a life of constant comparison. Our mountain of insecurities and inadequacies will always come out when we live this way. That's what happened with Leah and Rachel. The sisters certainly had their share of insecurities. Rachel was loved by Jacob, but had no kids at first. Leah quickly had kids, but wasn't loved by Jacob. Each one had what the other wanted and they agonized over it. Isn't this like us today, moms? We can have so much, yet it's not enough. We can get so wrapped up in what we *don't* have that we lose sight of what we *do*.

Let's talk about Leah, Jacob, and their relationship as husband and wife. What can we learn from them?

Leah's marriage to Jacob was hardly the romantic love story we fantasize about, but it was indeed a love story of even greater significance. As mentioned earlier, Jacob was a fugitive of sorts – running from his angry twin who wanted him dead. Jacob arrived at his Uncle Laban's house, fell head over heels for Rachel, and wanted to marry her pronto. With no money to his name, Jacob agreed to seven long years of hard manual labor as a dowry to marry her. This was far beyond the ordinary amount, but Jacob said yes because he loved her so much. He made an honorable deal with his uncle. He worked. He sacrificed. He waited patiently for Rachel. See, Jacob wasn't all that bad. They have a great love story so far, until their wedding night, when Jacob was tricked into marrying the wrong sister (who was heavily-veiled). The wedding custom at the time was for the bride and groom to be separated until after the festivities. Can you imagine being Jacob and making that discovery after the party was over? What in the world? The con worked. Jacob married the ugly sister, and then quickly agreed to work another seven years for Rachel, the love of his life. Did Jacob ever love Leah? Not really. Did Leah crave for her husband's attention and affection? Of course she did. But, his heart was set on Rachel. So how did Leah endure such a marriage? What was that like for her? In my mind's eye, I can't help but picture a lonely Leah feeling unvalued and unappreciated – maybe even invisible. Do you feel that way sometimes as a mom and wife? Perhaps you can relate to Leah on some level. I don't have all the answers, but here are some basic things I want us all to remember.

For starters, it's not uncommon for wives and moms to feel lonely inside our marriages sometimes. Marriage and motherhood bring with them a lot of hidden struggles and unanticipated challenges. Every marriage and relationship will face hard times, including periods where unexpected feelings of loneliness and/or disconnect arise. These are not things we anticipate on our wedding day when we marry our BFF, but they happen. We don't ever imagine feeling disconnected toward the man we made vows to or the family we're raising, but many of us feel that way sometimes. We can live together, eat together, watch TV together, and share a bed with one another, yet still feel lonely. We can share intimate physical spaces in our homes but lack emotional intimacy. Living with someone doesn't guarantee connection, and sharing a home doesn't guarantee sharing a life. I've noticed this in different seasons of my own marriage and parenting.

Let me just say this: There are no shortcuts to a happy marriage. There are no quick fixes or easy answers. Relationships are hard and complicated because people are hard and complicated. There are so many factors that contribute to breakdowns in any relationship. I can't possibly address everything here, but I do want to give you some food for thought. Here's what I know for sure: We can't control other people's behavior. We can't control our spouse or our children. We are ultimately only responsible for ourselves – our own words, behavior, and what we allow to take root in our heart. Why is that last one so important? Because what takes root will grow fruit. For Leah, what likely had taken root in her heart included jealousy, bitterness, anger, contempt, and resentment. I have related to some of those things at different times in my marriage. Have you? The truth is, our flesh gets us in trouble, moms. Nothing good comes when we're *filled with* and *acting on* any of those hurting emotions. When our ugly emotions go unchecked, watch out. They have no limits and we can easily make things worse instead of better. There are unintended consequences to everything we say and do. What attitudes or feelings might be developing in your heart toward your husband or your kids? It's important to know them, confess them, and ask God to help us release them.

God is always after our hearts. He wants to shape our hearts and develop our characters more than he wants to offer us quick solutions. He cares more about building our characters through marriage than building our comfort. Character development isn't easy, but it's necessary if we want to become strong women of faith.

If you're feeling lonely or disconnected in your marriage, will you ask God to show you what's behind those feelings? Will you be brave enough to ask Him to reveal your role in them, if any? Get curious and ask the deeper questions. A good place to start: What am I feeling? What are the facts? What am I believing about my partner? What else might be true about what's going on? Why are we no longer connecting or working like a team? When did I notice things changing? What's going on in our own worlds that may be a factor? I'll add, whatever initial answers you come up with aren't the only answers. There's more. Trust me. Dig deeper. We're often so focused on our own pain and insecurities that we lose sight of or are insensitive to our spouses' pain and insecurities, which are a whole other part of the equation.

Leah went through some hard and painful moments during her marriage, and it showed in the sad names she gave her children. With the birth of each baby, she hoped her husband would love her, but he didn't. When she gave birth to her fourth son, she decided to name him Judah, which means "this time I'll praise God." The progression of the names she chose to give her sons is an indication of how, over time, God was able to heal her broken heart and give her one that could be fully devoted to Him. Leah developed a loving relationship with a caring God who saw her and was moved by her sorrow. God noticed her and met her in the depths of her pain, rejection, and loneliness. In the end, the unloved Leah didn't find love in her husband, but ultimately, found love from the Lord. God's pursuing love was unlike anything else. Nothing else tasted the same. The truth is, if we can find God in our loneliness and emptiness, then we can find Him anywhere. God filled Leah's heart with His love and it changed her. She praised God not for her pain but *through* her pain. Leah may have felt rejected and unloved by her husband but never by God.

God never rejects his children. Leah's identity was ultimately built on God's love for her, rather than her husband's. In the end, how God saw Leah was infinitely more valuable to her than how Jacob saw her. This story shows us God has a special affinity for those who feel lonely and overlooked. Just like God was generous and attentive to Leah when Jacob wasn't, He is generous and attentive to you when others may not be. Leah sought the Lord in the midst of her loneliness and ultimately found God's love to be the love she needed. It's all she needed.

Remember the famous line from Jerry Maguire, when he tearfully tells his wife, "you complete me"? Jerry walks into his living room and admits how much he loves and misses her, and how life isn't complete without her. It's a beautiful sentiment, it really is. But the real truth is this: Neither our husbands, nor our kids can complete us. Only Christ can do that. Our spouse can't be our everything. First, it's a weight he's not designed to carry. Second, our spouse simply can't meet all our expectations. He's not perfect, and therefore will always fall short. Guaranteed. If we are trying to fill a void in our own heart with the love of another person, we are setting ourselves up for disappointment every single time. We all have a God-sized hole in our heart that only He can fill. If you ever notice yourself becoming disappointed because your spouse is not fulfilling all your life's hopes and dreams, I encourage you to do as Leah did and turn to God.

Here's a question I have wondered about Leah's story: Do you think that perhaps she idolized her marriage? I'll admit, it's sort of a strange thing to ponder, but I do wonder about it. Why? Because I think we all do, to some extent. The word *idol* is used a lot in the Old Testament; the early nation of Israel was always getting in trouble for their idolatry. They were constantly turning their backs on God, and embracing all sorts of other things – lesser things. We do the same thing today, and maybe we don't even notice. In simple terms, an *idol* is a thing that's first and foremost in your heart (that is not God). It doesn't have to be a "bad thing". Idols can actually be good things that we make into God-things. Idols could be the things you love most, the things you obsess over, sacrifice for, devote yourself to, the things that bring you the most security. I promise you, there are things fighting to be top priority in all our hearts. Could an example be our marriages? Yes, it could. It could be all sorts of things: our kids, our appearances, our jobs, our money, etc. It's usually something we're so preoccupied with that if we ever lost it, our lives would shatter. This is why God wants us to put Him first, above all else. We were made to worship; if we don't worship Him, we'll worship something else. I love my husband and kids, but I don't want to worship them.

Nothing and no one is more worthy of our attention and affection than Jesus. Yes, we need people. Yes, we're made for connection. First with God, *then* with people. Vertical first, horizontal second. It's important we get the order right. It symbolizes the cross and our need for God if we're going to have any chance at doing human relationships right. Ask God to search your heart in this moment. Are you prioritizing your marriage or kids above your relationship with your Maker? People, spouses, friends, and family will all disappoint us. A relationship with God never does. Maybe you need some time to meditate on this. Ask God to soften your heart to whatever He may be saying to you right now. What are you prioritizing?

I don't know what you're experiencing in your marriage right now, or if there are feelings of loneliness and emptiness, but it's only natural that we try to fix things on our own. I bet Leah did that. I bet she tried everything she could think of to get her husband to love her, but nothing worked. We too will reach for things to fill the void. Moms, God wants to meet you in your emptiness and fill that void. He promises that if we seek Him, we will find Him.

Until then, here are some practical things I recommend *not* doing in marriage if you're feeling disconnected from your partner:

- Don't ignore or sweep issues under the rug.
- Don't isolate or detach from your partner.
- Don't stay silent and pretend the problems will go away.
- Don't avoid or delay important conversations to avoid conflict.
- Don't self-medicate to soothe (overeat, drink too much, binge TV, etc.).

- Don't look for distractions to avoid what's really going on.
- Don't find negative ways to get your spouse's attention, like argue and blame.
- Don't maintain an image of a happy wife when you're hurting.

Here's what you *can* do:
- Have honest conversations about what you're noticing or sensing when it comes to your connection.
- Make your needs known.
- Approach conversations with curiosity, love, and compassion rather than anger, impatience, and blame.
- Make it a point to actively move toward each other.
- Forgive and ask for forgiveness as often as needed.
- Aim for meaningful interactions and points of connection on a daily basis.
- Pray for God's wisdom and direction.
- Seek professional help if needed.

Leah's life wasn't perfect, but in the end, the emptiness she felt in her marriage was replaced by her love for the Lord. In the words of Whitney Houston, He became her "greatest love of all." She may not have been loved well by Jacob, but she was perfectly loved by God. He alone healed her deepest wounds and filled her heart to overflowing. Jacob may have settled for her, but she didn't settle. She set her eyes on higher things and settled into a deeper identity as a child of God. God desired her like no man could. The God who saw her, heard her, and met her in her loneliness is the same God who sees you, hears you, and loves you too. Do you know that kind of love?

Here's a reflective activity you might want to try to rekindle the connection with your first love. Close your eyes, take a deep breath, and bring to mind the early days of your faith. When did you first encounter the love of God? What do you remember? Step into those feelings and allow yourself to relive the experience. Or perhaps, reflect on a memory from a recent time when you encountered God's presence. What was that experience like? How did it make you feel? What impacted you most about that moment? What did you learn about Him and about yourself? I hope you use some of these questions to help you recall a few of your God moments. This is an exercise you can return to in times of loneliness or emptiness, or when you are feeling unloved. You are so loved.

In the end, God created something really beautiful in and through Leah and her seven kids. It was from Leah's lineage, not Rachel's, that our Savior was born. That's incredible! The Light of the World came through Leah's son, Judah, a child she conceived with Jacob and whose name means "praise God."

Jesus said He's the Light of the World. He came to rescue us. When we *know* the Light of the World, we no longer live in darkness. Leah was brought out of her darkness – her dark thoughts, loneliness, emptiness, and feelings of not being loved. God's light revealed truth to her like it reveals truth to us. We are God's most treasured possessions, made in His image to love Him and be loved by Him. He's the missing piece in all of our lives. We can't fill our voids with anything else. Everything besides God is temporary and imperfect, including the love of others. No other person – not our spouse, not our children – is designed to complete us or make us whole like God is. Without embracing His love, we'll always be lacking.

Chapter 8

SOS *for the* Worried MOM - *Jochebed*
(Exodus 1 and 2)

I remember the time I took my kids to *Boo at the Zoo* around Halloween time. My daughter, then just five years old, was dressed as Snow White. My son was a penguin. Snow White insisted on wearing her plastic, high-heeled "glass slippers," which matched her puffy tulle dress. Though it seemed like a bad idea in my mind, I *let* her do it.

I remember the time my then 12-year-old son called me from school and asked me to bring his mouthguard to football practice, otherwise he'd have to sit out during the game. I *let* him. I think about the many times I've let both my kids leave the house on rainy days without an umbrella or jacket. Though it always seems like a bad idea in my mind, I *let* them do it anyway. Was I worried about my daughter's little feet in heels at the zoo? Was I worried about my son having to sit out the football game after waiting two years to play? Do I still worry about colds and flus and wet heads? Yes, yes, and yes. What's my point? Even though I worry, I've learned it's not only good but *necessary* to slowly release my kids to their own choices as much as possible and as early as possible. I know that it's the calluses and consequences that hold the life lessons they'll remember.

Now, I consider myself a decent enough parent with the good sense to know not to leave my kids to their own devices *all* of the time. There is no "all of the time." That would be nuts! But to "let them" do for themselves and decide for themselves whenever possible is key to their growth. Even if…? Yes, even if. Because moms, sooner or later, ready or not, willing or not, we must release our children into the real world. That's part of our mom role – to give them roots to grow and wings to fly. And yes, chances are we'll worry every step of the way, because a mother is always a mother, even when her kids are all grown up. It's a constant feeling of holding on and letting go, isn't it?

If you're a worrier, I get you. I see you. I *was* you. After all, worry makes sense. There's so many things to consider and choices to make, and where there's choice, there's worry. That's what making choices do to us. The process of making a decision (any decision) either has us doubting the choice we're leaning toward (because maybe there's a better way), or worse, leads us to think we're actually getting it wrong. The fact that moms worry so much already says something about us. It says we care about so many things:

Allergies, bullying, cavities, or delayed speech. Are they eating too much McDonald's? Am I failing as a mom? What about their grades? Should I homeschool? Are those heavy backpacks causing injuries? Wear your jacket! Did I put the kitchen knife away? What's their life's purpose? Medications. Nap schedule. Did I shut off the oven? Pool safety and playground politics. Why is it so quiet? Rap music. Too much screen time? SATs. Who are they texting? Are they wearing clean underwear and eating their veggies? Drinking enough water? What about X-Ray exposure, YouTube exposure, school on Zoom? Whew! That's a lot on the brain and hardly an exhaustive list, even though I ran through the entire alphabet.

Enter Jochebed. She's the biblical mom who comes to mind when I think about the topic of worry. Jochebed is the mother of Moses (plus Aaron and Miriam). She gave birth to her kids during a very troubling time in ancient Jewish history – a time when the people were slaves in Egypt. The Hebrew people were many and this worried the pharaoh, so he oppressed them. He thought the Jews would one day outnumber the Egyptians and revolt, so he forced them to do manual labor under cruel conditions. The catch was this: The harder they worked, the more kids they had. Their families grew like crazy. There were so many that at one point the pharaoh passed a ruthless order – every Hebrew boy under the age of three would be killed. All of them.

This was an attempted genocide of all Jewish babies. Can you imagine being the Hebrew mom of a baby boy during that time? What would typically be a time of cheerful celebration and anticipation was a time of overwhelming loss, grief, and mourning. I can't even fathom the collective suffering.

It was around this time that Jochebed showed courageous faith. After giving birth to baby Moses, she hid him for three months until she could no longer silence his cries. She placed her baby in a papyrus basket and released him among the reeds, along the bank of the Nile. Brave move for this brave mom. It's interesting to note the word used for the basket she placed him in is the same word used for the ark that Noah built. Just like God rescued Noah and his family, He saved baby Moses.

There's so much to wonder about when it comes to Jochebed. What was she thinking? Was she scared? Did she worry about her baby and his chances at survival? What words did she pray over him before she placed him in the river? What if the "wrong people" found him? Or worse, what if no one found him at all? What if he drowned? What about animals and predators? Did she worry the basket might tip over with a squirming baby in it? We don't know for sure if she was plagued with worry and to what degree; the Bible doesn't tell us. What we do know and what we can learn is that Moses's mom acted – and then waited – in faith, despite her level of worry. So what does that look like for today's mom? What does it look like to trust God with our worries?

I know what it looks like when I don't trust God: I worry about the daily things that directly impact me, whether big or small. I worry about things like my health, family, home, finances, but I especially worry about my kids. I worry about their present day and the future to come. Is this the right place to raise our family? Do I homeschool or send them to public school? What about private school? What college will they go to? How will their current friends influence them? What books are they reading? Are they good drivers? How is social media and technology affecting them? What about the political, progressive, conservative influences? Sexual identity? Young pregnancy? Drugs, alcohol, vices? Yes, I worry. And the more I think about these things, the more they consume me.

Essentially, when Jochebed released her son into the water, she revealed to us what she believed in her heart, "not *my* will but *yours* God." Let's take a moment to really let that sink in. That's probably one of the hardest things to say about anything in life, let alone our kids. However, I truly believe this is the heart attitude and posture God wants from all of us. A heart that is truly surrendered to God's will and way. A heart that trusts God more and worries less. A heart that *acts in* faith and *waits with* faith.

I'm on the cusp of releasing both of my young adult kids into the world. It's within reach and I'm not sure if I'm ready. My friends who are already in that season tell me it's a sudden loss they didn't see coming – even though they saw it coming. The emotions are plenty: there's sadness, worry, concern, worry, pain, and worry. Did I mention worry? Worry is the universal love language we share as moms. Aren't we lucky? The moment we birth our babies, we birth along with them a side of worry and a never-ending stream of questions that go with it. Is my baby okay? Is she eating okay? Is she sleeping too much? Do I breastfeed or bottle-feed? Is she growing and reaching healthy milestones when she's supposed to? Is she talking, walking, potty training when she's supposed to?" Many of us worry and worry and worry, and we just can't help it. It comes with the job. If this is you, welcome to motherhood, where we always worry because we never stop caring.

The Bible doesn't tell us what Jochebed felt when she released baby Moses into the water. It simply tells us that she did (release him). The Bible doesn't tell us what she felt when he was later adopted into and raised by the royal family. It simply tells us that he was. In all that time, over all those years, I wonder what Jochebed thought about. Did she worry about her son? Did she worry she'd never get to see him or hold him again, or sing to him or tell him she loved him? Did she worry he'd forget her and what she had taught him? Would he forget his humble beginnings and Jewish roots? Forget his mom's adoring face, her snuggles, and soft kisses? Releasing him was an act of faith on his mom's part. Releasing our own kids in due time is an act of faith on our part – or it can be an act of worry if we let it be.

Jochebed had no guarantee her plan would work. She didn't know what the results would be or what would come of her son. She was a Jewish slave living under oppressive rule with no money, means, prestige, or power. She simply did what she could and acted in faith. The truth is, not much has changed, moms. We can't know for certain our children's futures, either. We can't control every outcome. There are no guarantees. Like Jochebed, many of us moms live enslaved – not by oppression – but by our worried mindset. Is this you? Are you constantly worrying or anxious about your kids? Are your looping negative thoughts controlling and dominating you? Are you enslaved to worry? Maybe you've never thought of it in this way. Are you willing to? Our emotions can easily get the upper hand if we're not careful. You might say you've tried everything to rid yourself of worry and nothing has worked. You may believe the worry is just too big and shows up way too often. You may be under the impression that that's just the way it is. Well, I'm here to tell you there's a better way to live than bound by worry.

The antidote to worry is always faith. Yes, faith. Not the kind of faith that's passive and sits idly by doing nothing, but an active faith that interrupts our worry patterns *on purpose*. It's the kind of faith that requires us to put something into action – a truth, a belief, a promise God has given us. It requires us to practice something we know is true about God. Passive faith pays lip service to what you believe; active faith moves on what you say you believe.

Passive faith says "I know I need to _____" (worry less, trust more, pray more). Active faith decides "I will and am committed to _____" (worrying less, trusting more, praying more) and making that a daily practice. Here's a journaling activity you might find helpful. It's a good starting point.

ACTIVITY: Take out a sheet of paper and make two columns. You can use your phone or your choice of technology. In one column, write "I BELIEVE," and in the other column, write "I REFUSE TO BELIEVE." Let's begin with acknowledging what you're worried about. Bring things to mind, identify them, and then agree to set them aside for a few moments. You can return to them later. For now, we want to practice shifting our focus from what worries us to the truth about what God says *about* the things that worry us. For example, my worry at the moment has to do with my kids' futures – like their choice of college and career (and the campus culture and values that come with that), their friends, and any vices they may come across along the way. I sometimes worry about the decisions they'll make (and won't make) that could help or hurt their futures. Future worry is a big, recurring one for a lot of us moms. Whatever season you're in with your children, it's likely future focused. We tend to think "If X happens, then Y will happen," or "If X doesn't happen, then Y will never happen." When the things we can't control become our focal point, we naturally worry. But God doesn't want us to live with constant worry. He gives us His Word to remind us of the bigger picture.

Let's return to your columns. Write down what you believe and what you refuse to believe. For example: "I believe" is what you know for sure as it relates to God. I believe ____.

- God is Faithful and Sovereign in every situation.
- God is with me and will guide me when I don't know what to do.
- God wants to exchange my worry for His peace.
- God wants me to trust Him with the many things I can't control.
- God wants me to grow in the image and likeness of Christ, and worry plays no part in that.

In the "I refuse to believe" column, write down what you're choosing to take a stand *against*. Make a list of at least five things. Avoid inspirational sayings or quotes and instead, dig deeper for something truly meaningful and rooted in truth. I refuse to believe _____.

- I'm in this alone.
- This struggle is in vain.
- I can't overcome whatever comes my way.
- God has abandoned me.
- I can't.

Now that you've done this exercise, what stood out to you? How can you continue to affirm and contend for what you believe? How do these statements help you lean into faith? What attribute of God can you meditate on when your biggest worry creeps up? How can you put your worry in its place?

There are many wonderful verses in Scripture that address worry. Something I recommend is using the concordance, which is a valuable tool in the back of your Bible. The concordance is a special index that contains significant words used in Scripture, followed by references where that particular word is found. What does God have to say about "worry"?

- Philippians 4:6-7 "Do not be anxious about anything, but in every situation, by prayer and petition, with thanksgiving, present your requests to God. And the peace of God, which transcends all understanding, will guard your hearts and your minds in Christ Jesus."

Another translation of the same verse says, "Don't fret or worry. Instead of worrying, pray. Let petitions and praises shape your worries into prayers, letting God know your concerns. Before you know it, a sense of God's wholeness, everything coming together for good, will come and settle you down. It's wonderful what happens when Christ displaces worry at the center of your life."

When reading verses from the Bible, I recommend looking up the same text in different translations. Sometimes a passage can become so familiar over time that it loses its impact. A different translation can help bring it to life again as it hits you differently.

Here are some added verses that speak to worry, which I hope can encourage you.

- John 16:33, Jesus says, "I have told you these things, so that in me you may have peace. In this world you will have trouble. But take heart! I have overcome the world."

Moms, the key words here are "in me." Deep peace is available when we live *in Him*. The good news is that we don't have to let our circumstances dictate our level of peace. A relationship with God gives us the peace we long for, a peace this world doesn't offer. God is the solid rock on which we stand. All other ground is sinking sand.

- Matthew 6:34, Jesus says, "Therefore do not worry about tomorrow, for tomorrow will worry about itself. Each day has enough trouble of its own."

Moms, God wants us to focus on God's provision in the here and now, rather than on what *may* or *may not* happen tomorrow. Don't miss what He's up to in your life today! He strengthens and equips us each day for what's needed right then. Afterward, He asks us to rinse and repeat. He will help us tomorrow with what's needed and wanted tomorrow.

- Matthew 6:27, Jesus says, "Can any of you by worrying add a single hour to your life?"

Moms, our worrying doesn't accomplish much. It isn't effective and it doesn't yield good results. It's a pattern God wants us to break with His help as we learn to surrender our worries to Him.

By the way, the list of passages goes on. There are so many verses that straight up tell us not to be afraid or anxious, not to let our hearts be troubled or discouraged, and not to worry. Why? Because it's in our nature to worry. God, as a loving and wise parent, wants to personally speak to the most intimate parts of us. He knows us far better than we know ourselves. He knows we will naturally worry about the things we care about in life. I encourage you to come up with your own list of favorite verses that speak to your heart specifically. Write them out each day. Meditate and reflect on them. Journal and commit them to memory. Also, refer back to your "I Believe" and "I Refuse to Believe" journaling. It's a daily practice worth doing.

One of the many miracles in Jochebed's story is that when she released her baby into the water, and into God's hands, He brought Moses right to safety. The timing was truly impeccable. It just so happened that when Jochebed was at the river, the pharaoh's daughter was also there – ready to bathe. She saw baby Moses and rescued him. This was not a "chance encounter" or a "thank-you, universe" moment. The universe doesn't care about us. God, who created the universe, cares about us. He orchestrated and was sovereign over this divine intervention between a slave's baby and a rich king's daughter.

If you're anything like me, then you might be wondering about all the other babies who were not saved. So many baby boys were killed under this awful order. Did God not care about their little lives or the lives of their parents? Were their lives less significant? No. God chose to do something different in and through their lives than He did with Moses. Moses was saved and used by God to later free the Israelites from slavery. You likely know the epic story if you've read it or watched The Ten Commandments with Charlton Heston. The truth is, we all have a story to tell. Some stories are simple and quiet; some are grand and prominent. All of them are significant, and in all of them God is the hero, whether we acknowledge Him or not. I believe our loving, caring, and compassionate God met all the other moms in their time of loss and deepest heartache because that's what He does. God meets us in our painful circumstances. He brings comfort and healing to our deepest wounds. He walks with us and binds the brokenhearted. No one is immune to pain, loss, grief or heartache in life. God is ever-present in our time of need. Even when we don't feel Him, He's working. He's never as far away as we think He is.

So what can we learn from the brave Jochebed? It's natural to want the best for our kids. We of course want to protect them at all costs – from bad things, hard things, and most of all, from painful things. My gut tells me Jochebed must've worried about her son's safety when she sent him down the river, but she released Him anyway. She must've worried about his future, but she trusted God anyway. She must've worried about so much more, but she was faithful anyway. At our core, we always want our kids to be okay. Will they be okay, we wonder? Sometimes they will be and sometimes they won't be. And there's beautiful soul lessons to be learned from both.

Moms, many of us are tempted to constantly worry about something. Worry is what we know to do and we do it well. However, what I want you to know is that worry is a thief. It takes from us. It steals from us. It robs us of our peace and the present moment. We have to find a new pattern, a pattern of surrendering our thoughts, our worries, and anything that doesn't align with what God says. We must intentionally take our thoughts captive and renew our mind with what's true about God and what's true about us. Renew, renew, renew. That's the answer.

I wonder, how might your constant worry be blocking your communication with God today? Have you stopped hearing from Him, and feeling His presence? The only thing that stands between us and Him is the thing we're holding onto and refuse to let go of – could that very well be your worry?

If you're a Christian mom, you're not simply a Believer; you're a Receiver of new life. You've been given a new identity, power, and way of thinking and being in the world.

God has given you a new heart and put a new spirit in you, His Holy Spirit. Last I checked, worry never made it onto the Fruit of the Spirit list. That's not what's meant to grow inside of us. Do you know what is? Love, joy, peace, patience, kindness, goodness, faithfulness, gentleness, and self-control. God is always at work, taking us to higher levels of each. Worry has to take a backseat to what God is doing in us and through us.

So, how can we move away from constant worry and move toward lasting peace? It takes full-time effort to battle our nature, doesn't it? It requires us to practice walking more by faith and not by sight. I think sometimes we forget who we are, and act like we haven't been changed from the inside out. When our worry wins, we're letting sin win. When worry wins, we give it permission to move into the most sacred places within ourselves: our hearts and minds. Worry is one of the many things we can freely confess to God. When we confess all the ways we're not trusting in Him, it gives us an opportunity to invite Him in and ask for His help. He is always faithful to help us. That's the great news. God actually *wants* to help each one of us shed the layers of worry we wear as accessories.

I'll leave you with this, Worried Mom. I'm pretty sure most of us know firsthand what it feels like to worry, stand in worry, be in a state of worry, defend our worry, and thus, grow in worry. That cycle feels pretty familiar. How about we let that fade into the background and for a moment, stand in faith, act in faith, defend our faith, and thus, grow in faith? One way to begin this journey is to recall your own faith story – remind yourself of all the ways God has been faithful to you. Fix your eyes on Him. Invite His presence. Remember how much God has done for you already. Think about the times He was there for you when you maybe didn't see it or realize in the moment. Remember how He helped you keep going, how you felt His support and peace even when things around you didn't make sense. Remember the countless times He's carried you, and remember how He's always had your back. He has your back, Mom, He really does.

Chapter 9

SOS *for the* Praying MOM -
Hannah

(1 Samuel 1 and 2)

Have you ever thought of how you want to be remembered as a mom? I don't simply mean by all the fun things you did – which I'm sure were awesome – but who you were *being* to your kids in their day-to-day lives? What are you like? How would your kids describe you to their friends? Take a moment to think about this. If you're anything like me, your first inclination may be to gloss over these questions and continue reading. That's fair. I can't help but wonder, though, where else is that tendency showing up in your life? Remember, I'm not simply a mom offering you helpful tips and advice (to the extent you might think I am); I'm also a coach – your coach, if you allow me to be – during our time together in this book. As a life coach, more specifically, the Life Coach Mom, I naturally look for opportunities to push you a little, so that you can uncover deeper truths from within yourself and unlock *something*. Like what? Potential. Purpose. Possibility.

So I ask again, how do you *want* to be remembered as a mom? And how do you think your vision aligns with what your kids will *actually* remember? It reminds me of the time my husband and I took our two kids to Universal Studios in Florida. They were big fans of Harry Potter at the time, and pretty excited to trek across the country to walk the streets of Diagon Alley and ride the Hogwarts Express to Hogsmeade at Christmas time. We stayed in a nearby lakeside hotel and rode the ferry to the theme park each day. We went from park to park, rode the coasters, and enjoyed the immersive experience. Years later, I asked my kids what they remembered most about that trip, and their answer surprised me. They recalled the Cup Noodles we let them buy from the hotel lobby. They remembered the decadent chocolate dessert they shared at the steampunk-themed restaurant outside the park, and they remembered going to see Blue Man Group perform. Really? Those are the things they remember? Two of those three things I can find at my local Dollar Tree; I'm pretty sure we didn't need to go all the way to Florida for that. My point is this: What we *want* our kids to remember and what they *actually* remember don't always match up. The same applies to the question I posed above: How do we want to be remembered as moms?

Let's talk about Hannah from the Bible. Hannah is best known for being a praying mom – and a rather persistent one at that. She prayed all the time. When she was deeply troubled, she prayed. When she was in great anguish, she prayed. In the midst of her suffering, she prayed. How about you? Do you take the time to invite God into your everyday circumstances through prayer?

I don't think I'm quite like Hannah in this regard, but my mom was. She modeled prayer well. As her grown daughter, I'm grateful for her example. If I had to summarize what I remember most about my mom, it would be using the words inspired by Mark 12:30: "She loved the Lord her God will all her heart, soul, mind, and strength." These are the words inscribed on her memorial plaque at the cemetery. It captures the essence of who she was (and still is) in my mind and heart. Like Hannah, my mom was a prayer warrior. She contended and interceded for me throughout my entire life, including during the ten years I was away from my faith and needed it the most.

Let's dive deeper into Hannah's story and the lessons we can learn from her. For starters, we learn that Hannah is a woman of strong faith and character. She is patient in her suffering and persistent in prayer – both of which – are beautiful mom qualities we can strive for. Like many of the early matriarchs from the Old Testament (Sarah, Rebecca, Rachel, etc.), Hannah struggled with years of infertility. Even though each of these biblical moms were also praying moms who persevered, Hannah is especially recognized – not only for the *way* she prayed, but for the remarkable vow she made *while* she prayed. Hannah promised God that if she ever did have a son, she'd give him right back to Him. That's a hard thing for me to fully understand. What she promised was more than a baby dedication or baptism that we're used to seeing; Hannah literally promised to hand her son over to the temple priests to be raised up for God's purposes. Why would she do that? After all the years she waited to have a child, would she really just give him away? Yes… and that's what she did.

I have a dear friend whose son died at the age of two, due to cancer. She once shared with me how much Hannah's story resonated with her. After battling neuroblastoma, an infant cancer, Henry passed away and went to be with the Lord on Valentines Day. I know my friend's story doesn't exactly mirror Hannah's story, but it was in fact true, that she too returned her son to the Lord. If you've lost a baby at any time during any season, maybe this truth resonates with you as well. Could Hannah's story bring your hurting heart a bit of solace? I encourage you to read more about her.

For years, Hannah kept asking God for a son; year after year, nothing happened. She prayed, but no baby. She prayed more and still, no baby. Even when she was mocked by her fertile-myrtle sister-wife (polygamy was the norm), she continued to pray. That's remarkable. Peninnah (the sister wife) was a big bragger and made Hannah's life miserable, and yet, she continued to pray. I think I would've given up… I mean, what's the use of praying to a God who seemingly isn't doing anything? Who doesn't seem to be listening? I wonder if Hannah ever thought like this. Did she ever experience some kind of faith crisis while she waited? Did she ever doubt God's presence, His goodness, or maybe even His existence? Was she ever tempted to throw in the towel and just walk away? Scripture doesn't say. What we do know about Hannah is that she didn't stop praying. She kept at it. And though she had no child to show for all her years of praying, I bet she recognized she still needed God in her time of waiting. In the midst of her great pain and disappointment, she needed to connect with a loving God whose gentle voice could bring relief to the deepest places of her broken heart. Hannah was bold. She was fierce. She was specific when she prayed. Once, Hannah prayed so hard, and grieved with such trauma, that one of the priests thought she was drunk. Her lips were moving, but no words were coming out. Sober up, he told her. But no, that wasn't it.

We can't know for sure Hannah's exact words, but I imagine her prayers included phrases like, "God, where are You?" "Why are You neglecting me?" "Here's my pain. Do something." "I want so badly to have a son." "If You grant me one, I'll give him back to You. He'll be set apart for You. He'll be Yours, because ultimately, He *is* Yours."

What made Hannah remain constant in prayer? I suppose what kept her going was her very close, very real, and very raw relationship with God. Deep down, she must have believed wholeheartedly that nothing was (nor is) impossible for Him. What a great example for us today to never stop asking, seeking, and knocking. "For everyone who asks receives; the one who seeks finds; and to the one who knocks, the door will be opened," (Matthew 7:8).

Are you a praying mom? Do you regularly intercede and contend for your children in the here and now *and* for their futures? What kinds of things do you pray for? I'll admit, when my kids were younger, I'd pray sporadically about mostly physical things... sometimes I'd pray about weird things. I prayed for my kids to not get sick, to not get into trouble, to get an A on their test, to score a touchdown in football, to make the volleyball team, or for God to help them get out of the dumb things they did. Those prayers are welcomed – I'm not saying they're not, but as godly moms, could there be bigger, better, and ultimately, more *life-changing* prayers God wants us to pray? Are we missing out on those? Let's find out.

First, what is prayer? And is there a right way to do it? Prayer is simply a way to commune with God. It's how we, as created beings with a human soul, connect with our Creator, the One who created our soul. It's through prayer that we can simply talk to God about anything and every-thing. We pray to God to praise Him, thank Him, confess to Him, and ask for what we need. It's not about using fancy words to impress Him or anyone else. Prayer is more about the posture of our hearts. He invites us to be real, honest, and sincere.

Second, what are we doing when we pray? What does it accomplish? We're praying to the Father through Jesus, and in the power of the Holy Spirit. Why? God wants a relationship with us and He made that possible through Jesus. We were made for a relationship, *first* with Him, and *then* others. Prayer is not about giving God information He doesn't already know (because He does, in fact, already know). It's not something we should do as a last resort when we're desperate and all else has failed. And it's not a New Years resolution, it's about engaging in a relationship. It's like keeping a conversation going with a best friend. Prayer is how we as God's children simply talk to God, and move from being alone with our thoughts to handing our thoughts over to God. Whatever we long for and need, God has the answers. He IS the answer.

Third, what exactly do we say? Are there any rules or a specific formula? Christian prayer doesn't require that we use any pre-scripted words. So long as we're aiming to connect with the heart of Jesus, our own personal love language is welcome. We can pray in our home, at work, in our car, on a walk, in the elevator, or at the doctor's office. Location doesn't matter. We're not limited to praying in a temple or church because we don't need to pray in a place. We pray through a person.

Moms, we can't even think or imagine the height, width, and depth of what God is capable of doing in and through us. When we pray, we are praying to a God who can do more than we could ever ask for, more than we could ever think is possible. This is big stuff. We're not always going to be the perfect moms, but we can certainly be praying moms. Praying for our kids is a privilege – and it's not optional if we want to see change in their lives.

So, what are you asking God for? What *should* we be asking God for? For as long as we live, we as moms will always want the best for our kids. We'll forever be concerned about them. Our prayers will naturally include all the things we need and want and are thankful for in the physical world – a home, food, finances, a happy marriage, a happy child (or children), good physical, mental, and spiritual health, our kids' success at school, good friends and relationships, etc. All these things are good things to pray about. What I want to encourage us all to do is to reach even higher. There are other things that I think God would want us to pray for when it comes to our families – especially our kids – such as:

- For God to build in them a strong character and sense of purpose
- They discover their unique gifts early and put them into practice
- They come to know God at an early age
- The courage for them to do the right thing even when it's hard
- For our children's strengths to be developed and their weaknesses to be strengthened
- They learn to face tough days ahead
- For compassion, kindness, and generosity to grow within them

- Protection against culture and confusion
- They experience God's peace and presence on hard days
- They learn endurance and perseverance when when they fail

This is not an exhaustive list, but you get the idea.

Hannah eventually had a baby boy and named him Samuel, which means, "God heard." And because she was a woman of her word, she followed through with her vow. After Samuel was weaned, likely around the age of four, Hannah took her son to the temple and dedicated him to the Lord. It was there he was raised – like a child who goes to boarding school. Little Samuel started with light duties, wearing his own small tunic (clothing normally worn by a priest as he carried out his temple duties). He grew in the presence of God and served Him his entire life. He not only became a man of strong faith but a man of prayer as well, just like his mom. Samuel became one of the first major prophets in the Bible and anointed King Saul, and later, King David – two of the most prominent kings of Israel. It's rather remarkable that this baby boy, who seemed impossible to conceive, became instrumental in God's big plan of saving the world. (And by the way, God later blessed Hannah with three more sons and two daughters.)

From Hannah, we can learn that prayer changes things. Just like she persisted in prayer for her son, we too can do the same for our kids. We can be honest with God and not hold back our feelings, fears, hurts, hardships. We can bring all of our raw emotions to Him and surrender it all. God is big enough to help us carry everything on our plate.

I imagine that Hannah not only prayed to God on her darkest days, but she probably praised Him on those days too. How do we do that? Is it even possible? How do we find joy in our suffering? How do we worship God when we're hurting? The truth is, it's easy to praise God when life is good and things are going well. It's easy to praise Him for the beautiful things around us: the blue skies, sunrises, colorful sunsets, nature trails, and landscapes. However, if we can somehow also seek Him, also find Him in the hard times, then we can surely find him anywhere. How might God be working during your hard season? What might He be doing in and through your young kids, teenage kids, wayward kids, adult kids? In your infertility? While you're waiting for something important? How is He speaking to you in your pain, loss, worry, or discouragement? How is He giving you strength to endure one more day? How is this long waiting period shaping your character?

If you've ever prayed a long time about something and felt like nothing was happening, have you given up? It's natural for us to want to give up on prayer, on going to church, on God altogether when things don't seem to be changing. Perhaps though, it's possible that church is *exactly* where we need to be in the hardest of times. Gathering with our spiritual family shouldn't be replaced by our challenges. If you've been praying for something specific for a while and still have no answer, know that God isn't ignoring you. He may be asking you to wait – not alone, but in His presence with expectancy and anticipation. When we cry out to Him, even simply by saying His name, He's right there.

If you're new to the concept of prayer and want to start, here's how I suggest you approach it: with humility and simplicity. Find a quiet place to sit in stillness; set aside any distractions. Practice shifting your attention from yourself to God. Focus on Him. Invite His presence. Invite His peace. Begin releasing what's on your heart and mind. Be honest and vulnerable. It's not a performance. It's not about asking for stuff. God knows far better what we need than we do. If it helps, perhaps you might want to start a prayer journal and write down your ongoing prayers. Write down one or two simple sentences like, "Lord, my day is your day. Give me strength," or "God, I need your peace today with my kids," "Help me be," or "Help me grow." Take the posture of wanting what *He* wants and a willingness to receive what He wants to show you. Write your prayers down and track them. If it feels like God's not answering you, maybe it's because He's not giving you the answer *you* want. Keep seeking and asking questions; don't give up praying. There's no "magic formula," program to follow, or winning techniques. Simply, commune.

Whether you were raised in a Christian home or not, you're likely familiar with the Lord's Prayer, found in Matthew 6. It's how Jesus taught His disciples to pray, and one of the first prayers I learned as a kid, and maybe you learned it too. If you're anything like me, sometimes Scripture can become so familiar that it loses its impact. It's nice to circle back to it from time to time and ask God for a refresher. Let's use the Lord's Prayer as a template and break it down.

Matthew 6:9-13

(Matthew 6:9) Our Father in heaven, hallowed be your name,

Notice how this prayer starts – with having a right view of God. It begins with a reminder of who He is. When we pray "Our Father," it reminds us we can approach God like our dad. This is *whom* we're praying to. Prayer is about having a heavenly Father. What's more powerful than the God of the universe being our Father – making us His daughters? God wants us to get this right, because when we understand who He is, we can start to understand who *we* are. We're not simply sending prayers into the universe – the universe doesn't care about us. God, who created the universe, cares about us. God, who is holy and exalted above everything, who created the heavens and earth and makes all things new – He cares about you and me. That's whom we're praying to. One of the most beautiful things we can do is to spend time reflecting and reminding ourselves of who He is. When we do this, it causes us to worship him in a new way. If you want freshness in your prayer life, remind yourself of God's attributes. It's a game changer. Who is He?

(Matthew 6:10) Your kingdom come, Your will be done, on earth as it is in Heaven.

God ushered in a new kingdom – also known as a new way of life – through the life of Jesus Christ on earth. When the angel first appeared to Mary in a dream, he told her not to be afraid. He said she would have a Son, that His name would be Jesus, and that He would save His people from their sins. If you ever wondered what God's will is...that's His will. God is on a mission to save the world, one person at a time. When we pray "*Your* will be done," it's *His* will we're asking for, not our own. Our prayers should always be rooted in the will of God. We're saying, "God, we welcome Your plan, Your heart, and Your way in our current situation. We welcome all of what You're doing here on earth, because what other hope is there?" But let's be honest. We all have a will of our own, don't we? It's a battle sometimes – or maybe all of the time – to set aside what *we* want for what *God* wants. How do we do this? How do we come to accept His way over having our own way? The answer is: we yield. We are to hold what we want loosely in our hands and surrender it when asked. Yes, it's hard, but that's what praying for "His will" looks like. We're not always going to get everything we want, because that's not God's best. God doesn't give us everything we want, similar to how we don't give our kids everything they want. We have our reasons, and He does too.

I've worked in the TV industry for over 16 years. My heart has ached for big things in the professional world. I've dreamt for things that never happened and for things that haven't happened yet. You, too, have likely felt big disappointments in your own life or with your kids. We question God, ask Him, "Why aren't You making this happen? It's not working out how I want." However, rather than only focusing on how things *didn't* go, or how they aren't going as planned, we should also be spending time considering how God *is* working in our lives. When we don't get what we want, He's still working. What might God's will be for you in this season? How can you learn to embrace it more each day?

(Matthew 6:11) Give us today our daily bread.

With this line, we're acknowledging God is our provider and that we depend on Him for daily sustenance. We are declaring that we need Him every day. The truth is, we are physical *and* spiritual beings with real physical *and* spiritual needs. We have bodies that need to be nourished with food, and spirits that long to connect with our Creator. God meets both those needs and much more, because He is our source for everything.

(Matthew 6:12) And forgive us our debts, as we also have forgiven our debtors.

This verse reminds us that God is all about relationships. He's a big fan of healthy ones but sometimes, our sin gets in the way. We do things (and say things) that hurt others and ultimately ourselves. We need His forgiveness all the time. It's what brings us back into a right relationship with Him. Whatever we think our greatest need is, it's not that. Our greatest need is to return to God when we fail to reach the highest good, so we can return to right standing with Him. God restores us when we ask for forgiveness.

Are you in the habit of telling on yourself to God and asking Him for forgiveness? This is what is known as *confession*. It's a time for us to bring our flaws, failures, mistakes, and sin to Him. Why? It's not to shame or guilt us, but to acknowledge that sin plays no role in God's kingdom – our new way of life. Thank you, Lord, for the gift of forgiveness, which makes reconciliation possible!

This verse also reminds us that every time we pray, we should be forgiving others too. Receiving forgiveness from God should result in a forgiving spirit on our part toward others. We should be generous with our forgiveness, because we're the most forgiven people on the planet. God never struggles to forgive us, and we shouldn't hesitate to forgive others. It's what the Christian walk is rooted in; when we let unforgiveness take root in our heart, it blocks us when we pray. Unforgiveness keeps us from hearing God's voice and experiencing His peace. Is there unconfessed sin in your life that's keeping you from hearing God speak to you today? Jesus wants to set us free as we pray, so we can experience the fullness of His grace. It's hard to be free when we won't let go of a grudge, when we harbor anger, or when we hold onto bitterness. Who do you need to forgive?

(Matthew 6:13) And lead us not into temptation, but deliver us from the evil one.

This final phrase acknowledges that often we're weak when faced with temptation – and there's a whole lot of temptation around us, isn't there? It's easy to give in to lesser things or the 'wrong' things. That's why we need God's help, grace, protection, and deliverance all the time. Take a quick inventory of your life. In what areas are you weak and easily tempted? I guarantee we all have them. It could be in the physical realm or internal realm like in our thought life and emotions. Notice your thoughts right now. What lies are you <u>tempted</u> to believe about yourself? How often are you <u>tempted</u> to worry, stay angry, compare yourself, or put yourself down? How often are you <u>tempted</u> to think, say, act, or react in ways that don't serve you? How often are you <u>tempted </u>to do life alone and in your own strength because you believe God can't (or won't) help you? That He doesn't care or that He's forgotten you? Ask God to strengthen you against all these temptations and much more. Recognizing where we're weak is not a bad thing - it's actually a beautiful thing. It's in these places that God Himself shows up strong in our life, if we let Him.

So that's it, moms. That is how Jesus says we ought to pray. This is the type of prayer that pleases Him – one that magnifies God and advances His cause, His values, and His purposes. Prayer is not just about getting what we want, it's a time to enjoy sweet communion with our heavenly Father. Do your prayers do that? Do they magnify and promote what *God* wants, or what you want? If I'm honest, I've got the magnifying part down... but the other stuff? I'd rather pray really hard for me to get my way, not His.

I encourage you to simply talk to God. Pour out your heart. Tell Him about your day and your doubts. Tell Him about your worries and what keeps you up at night. Ask the hard questions. Tell Him how you're feeling. Confess your sin. Talk to Him. It can be as simple as, "God, thank you for being a loving Father who wants the best for me. I know your ways are always good. Help me be the kind of wife and mom you want me to be today, and help me to not compare myself to others. I confess, I struggle sometimes with patience and anger, but I know you can help me control my emotions. Forgive me for not turning to you more often. In Jesus's Name, Amen."

I pray that your prayer life can be a time of solace and rest for your spirit, as well as a sweet time of fellowship with your Creator. I encourage you to make it a daily practice – if it's not already – and see what happens in your faith walk. The truth is: A praying mom changes things, because prayer changes us.

For some simple prompts to help you get started, click
the link for my free resource www.mirellaacebo.com/free

Chapter 10

SOS for the Suffering MOM - *Bathsheba and Mary*

(Bathsheba - 2 Samuel 11)
(Mary - Luke 1:26-38 and Luke 23)

UGH. I hate it when things break or don't work properly, like my printer, car, tv remote, or my refrigerator that keeps beeping all hours of the night. Fortunately, when I need help, I know exactly who to call. He's the cute handyman who likes to flex and flirt while he fixes things - my husband. Julian has been called a "jack of all trades but master of none." He has a mindset that says, "If it's broken, I can fix it." I like that about him. He's not afraid to take things apart and put them back together again. And when he's not able to fix something or he's in over his head, he has the common sense to know when it's time to tap out and hand the job over to someone more qualified.

Moms, there's something pretty profound with this common sense approach. We all have specific people we call for help in our time of need. Am I right? We call the mechanic when our car breaks down – and we need help. We call the plumber when our faucet leaks – and we need help. We call our hairdresser when our hair turns gray – and we need help. Do we call on Jesus when we're suffering and need His help?

Suffering is a natural part of our lives and it takes many forms. Suffering can come in the form of worry, anxiety, depression, restlessness, or hopelessness. We can suffer from loss, physical health issues, mental health issues, financial crises, broken relationships, hard marriages, or hard children, to name a few. Sometimes, suffering is a direct result of something we did (or didn't do); other times, it's a result of what someone else did (or didn't do). Not all days are created equally, are they? Not all seasons are created equally, either. It's why I think to myself "a day without pain and suffering is a good day." Take it in. Savor it.

The two biblical women who come to mind when I think of suffering are Bathsheba, mother of Solomon, and Mary, mother of Jesus. Let's talk about Bathsheba first.

Bathsheba is a woman in the Bible who endured tragedy after tragedy after tragedy. It's impossible to tell her story without mentioning King David and his abuse of power and position over her. It's through his actions we get to know about her in the first place. In short, King David summons and takes advantage of a married Bathsheba one night. She gets pregnant, her husband is killed, and then her baby dies. All this in under a year. That is a whole lot of pain, betrayal, loss, and suffering. What in the world is going on? There's so much to take in. How does someone endure even one of these tragedies, let alone all of them back to back?! The answer: God's grace. God showed up for Bathsheba and redeems her devastating story. God didn't simply mend her broken heart, He did something new and amazing in her so she wasn't that broken person anymore. God doesn't always withhold pain from our lives if that pain can somehow accomplish His good purposes. Even though Bathsheba was wronged, God restores her and her story. He repairs sin's damage, and brings about something good because God can (and *will*) bring that kind of beauty from ashes so that nothing is wasted. Only He can bring joy from sorrow.

It's the same with us. God not only wants to meet us in our time of suffering, He wants to give us new and abundant life *in place* of suffering. Do you believe that's possible? Do you believe He can use the hard things you've gone through – or are going through right now – to help you grow beyond what you thought was possible? Well, He certainly can and He certainly will when we fully surrender to receive His help. That's one of the most beautiful promises God makes. Sin and sorrow never have the final say, God does.

Let's go deeper into Bathsheba's story and see what we can learn about suffering. Bathsheba was a beautiful woman, married to an honorable man named Uriah who was a loyal soldier in King David's army. Her dad and grandfather also held trusted positions for the king. One night while Bathsheba's husband was away at war, King David got up from his bed and strolled on the roof of his palace. What did he see? A lovely woman, bathing on her rooftop. He wanted her badly and couldn't resist. David summoned Bathsheba and forced her to commit adultery, which resulted in pregnancy. Then, King David concocted a plan to try and cover it up, but when that didn't work, he had Bathsheba's husband killed in battle. What started out as a small glance from King David turned to lust, abuse, betrayal, then murder… plus the loss of a baby soon after birth. That's what sin does. It can start out small at first but then slowly, it turns into more, causing a devastating chain reaction that leads to pain and suffering for self and others.

What a sad story. Scripture doesn't tell us a whole lot about Bathsheba or how she felt, but there is no doubt in my mind that she suffered as she mourned the loss of so much, including her husband and baby. Life as she knew it was over. One reckless moment led to a slew of tragedy and heartbreak that changed the course of her life.

No one is excusing David's criminal behavior. No one. It's clear that after time, he was experiencing his own mountain of suffering because of his sin. He was consumed with guilt and shame over what He'd done. One of the main things that stands out to me about King David is that even though he was the perpetrator in this story and perhaps didn't deserve mercy, God showed him mercy anyway. God was generous with him and forgave him. But then again, isn't that *so* God – to give and forgive beyond what we deserve?

God wants to do for you and me what He did for King David. God forgave him and took him back. Even after everything he did, King David is later described in Scripture as being "a man after God's own heart." At first glance, it might seem insulting and offensive to "excuse" a man for wreaking havoc on this woman. But the truth is that Jesus died so we *could be* forgiven for our sins, healed from our brokenness, and be rescued from eternal condemnation. He loves us too much to make us carry our sin, guilt, shame, and regret forever. Our shoulders aren't meant to carry all of that. Instead, He forgives so we can be released from our past and walk forward in freedom as changed people. God came to save sinners; we don't need to hide our sins from Him.

Mom, do you have guilt that is making you miserable? Does it contribute to some of your suffering? Our own secret or hidden thoughts can sometimes do that. They tyrannize us. They cause us to pull away from God, ourselves, and our loved ones, which creates even more suffering. Honestly, it's a great thing that God doesn't let us be happy when we do the wrong thing. Thank God we feel guilty when we sin. That internal heart conviction we feel is our healthy conscience, and it serves a redemptive purpose – it helps us get back on track. If you're suffering from a guilty conscience that's making you sick, relief is possible but can only be found in the arms of a forgiving God. David found relief when he acknowledged his sin and stopped trying to hide from it. Sin and pain are not the end of his story – redemption is. And that, right there, is good news, and should give us much hope.

One of the beautiful things about being in a saving relationship with Christ is that we don't have to stay stuck in our sin or our suffering forever. King David didn't stay stuck in his sin and Bathsheba didn't stay stuck in her suffering. God forgave King David and redeemed Bathsheba. He had a good plan for both of their lives that transcended their present pain. King David later married Bathsheba, and she became a powerful, influential queen and mother to King Solomon, another important person in Scripture. Bathsheba may not have had much choice in what happened to her – she didn't choose the tragedies of her life, but she did get to choose what she wanted the rest of her story to look like. By the end, her marriage to King David was full of affection, love, and respect. Plus, she's mentioned in the genealogy of Christ. God turned all things around for the greater good.

I don't know what you're suffering through and I hesitate to offer an explanation as to what God might be doing through it, but what I want to say is whether you've played a part in your present suffering or you are the victim,

God wants to meet you right where you're at and love you through it.

God is a God of love, grace, mercy, forgiveness, and restoration. God didn't forsake David or Bathsheba. He brought them together and gave them a rainbow baby (Solomon). *Rainbow baby* is an affectionate and loving term used by parents to describe the pregnancy after losing a child. Solomon not only grew up to be the wisest and wealthiest king over Israel at that time, but both David and Bathsheba were in the lineage of Christ. Jesus was born through their bloodline, which is pretty incredible. Who would've thought?!

The story ended with a humble and remorseful King David who lamented his actions and took full responsibility for what he did. He didn't hide his sin from God, he acknowledged it. He owned what he did and cried out to God for help. His heartbroken request to be forgiven and restored is recorded in Psalm 51.

God knows everything we're carrying as moms, as wives, and as women. He knows our deepest wounds, hurts, and longings; he knows all our questions and doubts. No suffering is beyond His reach nor beyond His gentle touch. Our job is to bring it all to Him, right now even, at this very moment. Bring your suffering and pain, anger and bitterness, wounds and hurts. God's spirit, His Holy Spirit, is powerful enough to lift and carry it, so you can be free. Doesn't that sound good? He forgives generously so we can be forgiving toward others – especially those who've hurt us. He wants to be gracious towards you so you can be gracious toward others.

Unlike the age-old nursery rhyme of Humpty Dumpty, where he ends up shattered and broken to the point that no one can fix him, nothing is too difficult or impossible for God to reconstruct. He can put anyone back together again. I believe God did that for both David and Bathsheba. David's sin was forgiven and Bathsheba's pain was ultimately redeemed so she could be restored. Neither of their pain was wasted.

Let's talk about our kids and how they, too, can be a critical source of *our* suffering. We may not imagine that to be true on the day they're born, but it is. To be a mother is a call to suffering sometimes. There's no better way to say it. Some moms suffer when our kids are born, when they leave the nest, everywhere in between, and then some. It's just our nature. When they hurt, we hurt. When they're in pain, we're in pain. When they're suffering, we're suffering. What better example of this is there than Mary, the mother of Jesus?

Mary was chosen by God to bear His son and raise Him. What an incredible honor. But as we know, her role didn't come without pain and suffering. As she would later find out, bearing God's son meant she would also bear the worst imaginable pain.

Let's dig into her backstory to see what we can learn.

Mary was a young and humble peasant girl living in a small village called Nazareth. She was minding her own business one day when suddenly, an angel appeared and told her God had a surprise for her: She was going to be pregnant soon and give birth to a baby boy! His name would be Jesus and He would be the Son of the Most High. Mary, a virgin, couldn't believe it at first, but later bursts with the good news. She quickly told her cousin Elizabeth, also pregnant, about the miraculous conception and how she felt like the luckiest girl in the world. Her song is recorded in Luke 1:46-55.

What stands out to me already about Mary is how happy she was about the baby that was to come. Granted, there was the fact that she was unwed and pregnant, which in that culture was a big no-no. She knew her pregnancy would bring immediate disgrace and public shame upon her, but there was no shame in saying "yes" to God and bearing His son. I believe her joy came from accepting this God-sized assignment for her life. I too remember the excitement for and anticipation of each of my kids when I was expecting. Very few things compare to that season of firsts: first positive test, first signs of a baby bump, first maternity outfit, first heartbeat, first time someone notices your growing belly, the first time you get to see your baby, hold your baby, and kiss your baby. I imagine Mary shared in some of those joys 100 times over, knowing her baby would be the greatest gift to mankind – to the extent she understood that. And because I know how Jesus's story goes, it's all the more heartbreaking to imagine what Mary went through watching his life unfold.

The crucifixion story is a brutal one. It was brutal for Jesus. It was brutal for Mary. Death on a cross was reserved for the worst of the worst criminals. Crucifixion was used by many people groups but was "perfected" by the Romans. The crucifix was essentially a torture device that inflicted severe amounts of pain over differing periods of time – some people died in hours, others after days. To be crucified was to die a horrific and violent death. Not to mention the public ridicule, while the naked body was on full display for all to see. I think Jesus's death pretty much exemplifies a mother's biggest fear and worst nightmare: to raise her child in a good home only to release him into the hands of the world, where he is destroyed. This, to me, is the bravest thing we can do as moms. We give our kids life. We love them, care for them, and keep them safe for as long as they're with us. But at some point, whether they're (we're) ready or not, we must let them go into the great big world and face all that it offers – the good, bad, and ugly. The world can be a beautiful place, but it can also be a scary and dangerous place – with a touch of hell once in a while. I imagine watching Jesus die was Mary's hell.

Mary had "released" Jesus into the world three years prior. He was teaching people, healing people, and amazing people with his wisdom and miracles. Everywhere He went, the crowds formed and followed. Some people loved Him and others hated Him. Eventually, he landed on the path of death, where he was first beaten and bruised before being hung on a cross to die. Mary was likely there for all of it. I imagine she witnessed Jesus' humiliation as he was dragged before Pilate for judgment and later whipped almost to death. I imagine she saw the angry mob and soldiers who spat on him and chanted, "Crucify him! Crucify him!"

The image of Mary at the foot of the cross watching her son die a slow death is so heart wrenching. Mary was no longer the same delighted teenager who carried the Son of Man in her womb. She is now almost 50 years-old with the wrinkles and worry lines that come along with motherhood. I can't begin to imagine the depths of her pain. Jesus was barely recognizable after being tortured and flogged by the Romans, but a mother always knows her child. She'd been His mom for 33 years, but she could do nothing to save Him in His most dire moments. She watched from a distance as His head – crowned with thorns – was slumped over, as He was waiting to die. Even though Mary knows her son is divine and that this is his earthly fate, she is still a human mother watching her son suffer. Had she watched in horror as the soldiers hammered nails into His hands and feet? Did the sound of each hammered nail pierce her heart? How did she do it? How did this not crush her?

In my mind, Mary is the mother who felt every raw emotion, and to the extreme: worry and fear, distress and agony, heartbreak and grief, overwhelm, and most definitely rage, to name a few. I imagine Mary was desperate to step in and stop the madness. What she wouldn't have given to rewind the clock, if she could've just had one more day to hold her son, to kiss him one more time. Jesus took his last breath and uttered his final words, "It is finished." His heart stopped, and I imagine hers did too, if only just a little. She knew He was gone.

Mary watched her son die. That alone brings unbearable suffering to a mom. But then, to watch him die a death by crucifixion – that's a mother's crucifixion too. The worst pain that could ever be inflicted upon her soul.

Jesus went to the cross voluntarily. He said "yes" to God's plan of salvation. In the garden of Gethsemane on the night of His arrest, He prayed, "Not *my* will, but *yours* be done." He didn't run from the cross and neither did Mary; they both faced it. What a lesson for us today as we face suffering.

If you're a mom, you've likely suffered along with your child in one way or another. We clearly can see how Mary experienced suffering in watching her son suffer. We will too. We suffer in labor, when they're sick, when we can't cure the disease, when they're hurting and we can't remove the injustice, when their friends walk away, when they cry and don't tell us why, when they're struggling and we can't make things better, when they're mistreated or bullied, when they pull away and rebel, when they make foolish choices that come with serious consequences, the list goes on.

King Solomon (Bathsheba's son) wrote in Proverbs 10:1, "A wise child brings joy to a father; a foolish son brings grief to a mother." (NLT) There's a lot of opportunities to grieve, aren't there, moms?

Yes, we live in a world where suffering exists and no one is immune to it. But suffering also calls out of us a strength we don't even know we have until it's right in front of us, and a perseverance we never knew was possible. That was true for Mary and it's true for us, too. Mary couldn't save her son from dying but she stayed with him until the end. When the rest of the disciples fled, she remained. I can only imagine how much her being there meant to Jesus in the midst of his suffering.

Here's the good news for the Christian mom: The crucifixion isn't the end of the story, the resurrection is. Mary's story of suffering doesn't actually end with tragedy; it ends with new life. Three days after Jesus's death, and to everyone's surprise, He rises. He comes alive again, and is still alive now, making all things new. Resurrection is just the beginning of the next chapter of life.

Two thousand years ago, Jesus walked out of an empty tomb in order to walk into the emptiness of our hearts. That's the gospel message. Because Jesus is alive, we can be transformed. Every aspect of our lives can be transformed the moment we believe and receive Him. God brings meaning and purpose to our days and He repurposes our pain and suffering so it no longer can destroy us. When we come to Him in full surrender and humility, acknowledging our sin and our need to be saved from ourselves, God moves in. He generously gives us the gift of

His Spirit, which includes a new identity, strength, power, and confidence. And this, moms, changes everything! We no longer walk through life alone once we allow God in. We no longer simply live and breathe and do life the same way as before. The beauty is we get to exchange our life for the life He has for us.

The truth about suffering is that it's something no one wants, but we're all pretty much guaranteed to experience. I think more often than not, we're asking God to remove our pain and suffering or to change our circumstances. And while He certainly can if He chooses to, it's more likely He wants to do something significant in and through our suffering to show the world who He is and what He can do. Maybe He wants to change us through our tough times so we come out stronger on the other side. Maybe He wants to wean us off of ourselves so we learn to lean into Him more.

Suffering isn't something we ought to rush to avoid or escape. Consider it an invitation to continue to find and embrace Jesus. Maybe facing our struggle and walking through suffering *with* Jesus, *is* the answer.

Mary is a great role model for us in our time of suffering. Her love for Jesus and her faith and hope *in* Jesus (and his divinity), is what helped her stand strong by the cross. Her example can help us too. How we respond to suffering matters. Our attitude toward hard times matters. We can either turn outward or inward. God knows what you're going through right now. He sees your suffering. He sees your pain. He just wants your mustard seed of faith, then He can do the rest.

Acknowledgments

Thank you God for your strength in this life.

Thank you to my husband and kids. You are everything to me.

About the Author

Mirella Acebo is a certified life coach and mom (a.k.a., *The Life Coach Mom*). She has over ten years of experience leading and teaching women in the area of self-development and spiritual growth. She is a teaching leader at an interdenominational Bible study where she lectures, leads seminars, and facilitates small-group discussions. Her passion is to help the everyday, busy mom re-discover who she is and what she wants in life - apart from her roles as wife and mother. She engages women in deep and meaningful conversations that help them get in touch with the parts of themselves they may have set aside for the sake of their family. Her gentle and nurturing approach brings support, encouragement, and clarity to the relationships that matter most.

Aside from her work as a life coach, Mirella is also a writer, actor, producer, and storyteller with over 15 years experience in the TV industry. She has appeared in many film, television, and national commercials. She and her family currently reside in Los Angeles, California.

You can stay in touch at
Mirellaacebo.com
Youtube: Life Coaching by Mirella
Instagram @lifecoachingbymirella

Next Steps

Thank You For Reading My Book!

I really appreciate all of your feedback and
I love hearing what you have to say.

Take two minutes now to
leave a helpful review on Amazon
letting me know what you thought of the book.

Thanks so much!
Mirella

Made in the USA
Las Vegas, NV
13 November 2023

80816126R00105